PERTHSHIRE'S POUND OF FLESH

TRUE TALES OF MURDER, REVENGE AND RETRIBUTION FROM PERTHSHIRE'S DARK PAST

Mark Bridgeman

Perthshire's Pound of Flesh © 2024. All rights reserved.

Copyright © Mark Bridgeman
All rights reserved. The right of Mark Bridgeman to be identified as the author of the Work has been asserted in accordance with the Copyright, Designs & Patents Act 1988.

This edition published and copyright 2024 by
Tippermuir Books Ltd, Perth, Scotland.

mail@tippermuirbooks.co.uk – www.tippermuirbooks.co.uk.

No part of this publication may be reproduced or used in any form or by any means without written permission from the Publisher except for review purposes. All rights whatsoever in this book are reserved.

ISBN 978-1-913836-43-6 (paperback).

A CIP catalogue record for this book is available from the British Library.

Project coordination and editorial by Paul S Philippou.

Designed by EMB Graphics, Aberfeldy

Co-founders and publishers of Tippermuir Books:
Rob Hands, Matthew Mackie and Paul S Philippou.

Text set in ITC New Baskerville 11/15pt.

Printed and bound by Ashford Colour Ltd.

This book has been printed in the UK to reduce transportation miles and their impact upon the environment. It has been printed to comply with the Forest Stewardship Council (FSC) Chain of Custody requirements and paper sourcing from responsibly managed sources.

PERTHSHIRE'S POUND OF FLESH

TRUE TALES OF MURDER, REVENGE AND RETRIBUTION FROM PERTHSHIRE'S DARK PAST

Mark Bridgeman

CONTENTS

Introduction

1. The Lovers Lane Killing
2. Five Shots, Two Murders, One Suicide
3. The Meggernie Murder
4. The Forgotten Killings
5. The Man Who Was Hanged Twice
6. The Bantam of Bovain
7. The Dying Murderer
8. The Killing of Janet Smith (Part One)
9. The Killing of Janet Smith (Part Two)
10. The Champagne (and False Teeth) Lifestyle
11. The Blairgowrie Murder
12. The Butler Did It
13. The Baron's Chauffeur
14. Highland Perthshire's Unsolved Mysteries
15. The Wild West Frontier
16. The Aberfeldy Riots
17. Assault with a Cut-Throat Razor
18. Where is Arthur Irvine?
19. The Blairgowrie Mystery
20. The Craigie Glassblower
21. Camp 21: Comrie's Wartime Secret
22. The Motiveless Murder (Part One)
23. The Motiveless Murder (Part Two)
24. Remembering Perthshire's Witches

Acknowledgements

INTRODUCTION

"Before you embark on a journey of revenge, first dig two graves" - *Confucius*

How do I follow The River Runs Red? That was a question I asked myself, as I painstakingly researched new stories for this edition. The answer, I decided, was to take the reader on a darker, and deeper, journey; plumbing the depths of the human psyche to explore the darkest of all our emotions – revenge.

The stories in *Perthshire's Pound of Flesh* encompass tales from across Perthshire, including Aberfeldy, Pitlochry, Blairgowrie, Crieff, and Perth itself. Revenge and retribution are the themes that weave their way through many of the stories. These motivations can take many forms, fuelled by anger, frustration, and desperation. There are notorious serial killers, infamous unsolved murders, desperate troubled murderers, and tragic tales of man's cruelty to man, all contained in this wallow through Perthshire's murky past.

Some of the darkest stories I have ever uncovered are contained over the following pages, including surprising links to Canada's most infamous unsolved cold case, the Moors Murderers and a 1970s serial killer who stayed at a Perthshire Hotel – with his victim.

There's a hint of the supernatural too, not to mention, perhaps, the darkest moments in Perthshire's past, it's zealous persecution of witches in the 17th century. The hounding and torture of these poor women (and it was mostly women) beggars belief to our modern sensibilities. For 'light relief' (if you can call it that!) the art of the conman is also explored.

A further thought crossed my mind while I was writing this book. Our personal understanding of the past, and the way that people lived their lives, isn't always told by the grand tales of Kings and Queens, or the history of large cities and world wars. I firmly believe we can learn more, and understand more, about the past, by examining the minutiae, of how ordinary people were forced to live, act, and behave. 'Inside Out History', I call it. What motivated their behaviour? What choices did they really have in their daily lives? How did the environment around them influence their conduct? Could any of the tragedies uncovered here in this book happen today?

I fervently hope that this exploration of the past not only entertains, but also provides a valuable link to the social history of our ancestors. It is certainly impossible to sympathise with, or justify, the behaviour of many of the unsavoury characters in this book. However, I hope

INTRODUCTION

we all, at least, gain a better understanding as the desire for revenge might just be lurking inside any of us. As Muhammad Ali, the former world heavyweight boxing champion, once said, "I believe in the eye-for-an-eye business. You kill my dog, you better hide your cat."

Mark Bridgeman

AUTHORS NOTE:

The story *The Killing of Janet Smith* previously appeared in serialised form within the pages of the Perthshire Advertiser in July 2020 and was subsequently adapted and broadcast on Canadian radio. The version included in this book, however, is an expanded and extended adaptation, containing new information not included in the previous version.

THE LOVERS LANE KILLING

Nineteen year-old Danny Kerrigan and his sweetheart, 17-year-old Marjory Fenwick, had decided to spend the evening together. The couple had been courting for eight months and were blissfully happy. Danny Kerrigan was an apprentice glazier, with MacLeod's in Perth, and a promising junior footballer with Scone Thistle. Marjory was employed at Campbell's Confectionery Works in Perth. It was Wednesday 15th August 1935, and the weather for the past week in Perth had been sunny, warm, and dry.

The couple discussed how to spend their evening together. Marjory suggested *Our Little Girl*, the latest Shirley Temple film, showing at the recently opened Playhouse Cinema in Perth. Danny had chosen *The 39 Steps* on their previous visit to the Playhouse, so it was Marjory's choice this time. However, as the evening was so balmy, the couple eventually agreed on a walk in the hills above the city instead. It was a decision that would end in tragedy and with a crime that would shock the nation.

Danny left his house in Union Street in Perth, and met Marjory, who lived in Dovecotlands in the city, and the pair headed up, through Cherrybank, towards Buckie Braes, just behind the Craigie Hill Golf Course. Marjory promised her parents she would be home a little after 10pm.

The couple walked and talked, heading eventually along Cuddies Strip, a winding track lined with gorse bushes, well known as a 'lovers lane' among local courting couples. After an hour or so they decided to sit down, about 250 yards from the stile that led down towards the Dunning Road. Danny had some photographs, in his pocketbook, which he had intended to show Marjory. The couple laughed and chatted until they heard the clock from Perth Academy chiming 10 o'clock through the warm night air. Marjory, on hearing the time, told Danny, 'It's about time we were getting home now', and the couple headed down the hill, arm in arm.

They appeared to be completely alone. They could see no one in front or behind them on the path. Suddenly the peace of the night was shattered as the sound of a gunshot rang through the air. The shot seemed to be incredibly close by. Marjory distinctly felt a vibration, as the bullet whistled past her right ear. Stopping in their tracks, the pair looked at each other, Danny seemed to regain his composure quickly, and wryly joked, 'You aren't going to faint are you, Marjory?'

Before she could answer him, another shot echoed through the still night air. Danny Kerrigan fell violently backwards, his body crashing to the path. Marjory instantly kneeled beside him, 'Danny, Danny', she cried.

He was moaning audibly, and his face was covered in blood.

Out of the blue, a man appeared behind her, stepping out from behind the gorse bushes. He was wearing a dark jacket and cap, with a handkerchief secured over the lower part of his face. Marjory, even in the half light, became acutely aware of his 'glaring eyes'.

'What are you doing?', she asked, in a state of shock and apprehension.

The man said nothing. Made uneasy by his sudden appearance, she turned and ran towards the stile, which was 250 yards down the path. 'I'm going for help', Marjory shouted as she ran. Without speaking the man ran behind her, catching her just as she placed  her right foot on the stile. He grabbed her from behind, putting one hand over her mouth, and threw her, face down, to the ground. Before she could react, he had his body weight on her, holding her down with his foot or knee in her back. Producing a handkerchief from his pocket, he tied her hands behind her back and dragged her into the bushes. Once there, the man untied her hands again, but only to allow him the opportunity to remove her clothing. Terrified, Marjory pretended to faint, while the man gagged her with her own suspender belt, re-tied her hands and, with his hand over her mouth so she could barely breathe, assaulted her. He then bound her feet together, gathered up her clothing, and, without uttering a word, walked off, back in the direction of Danny's body still lying on the path, 250 yards away.

Lying face down, her head turned to the side, Marjory watched in horror as the man fired another shot into Danny's lifeless body. He then covered the bloodstained face of his victim with a second handkerchief, removed Danny's pocket-book, containing approximately 12 shillings, and vanished into the night.

It took Marjory approximately 30 minutes to free her hands and feet. Once she had done so, she stood up but could not see any of her clothes or underwear apart from her swagger coat. Quickly wrapping the coat around herself, barefoot and with the handkerchief still tied to one wrist, she headed down the hill towards Cherrybank and the safety of the town, too fearful to go back for Danny, in case the man was still hiding in the bushes.

At the end of Buckie Braes Marjory bumped into another young couple, Mr Spence and Miss Ewen, also out walking. They were startled by her appearance. Marjory was dressed only in her coat, was barefoot, and obviously in distress.

'Can you help me, mister', she pleaded, 'There's a man in the Cuddies Strip. He shot Danny Kerrigan and took my clothes off.'

The couple, realising the seriousness of the situation, acted immediately. Spence went to telephone for the police and Miss Ewen knocked on the door of a house in Cherrybank Road, where they borrowed some clothes for Marjory and awaited the arrival of the authorities.

At around midnight, when the police arrived, Marjory was able to lead them back to the spot where Danny's body was lying, unmoved, on the ground. At this stage Marjory was still not certain whether her sweetheart was alive or dead.

Following the discovery of the body, a large search party was hastily organised and police officers, armed with torches, combed the Buckie Braes and nearby fields. However, in the days before the development of Perth to the south and the building of the dual carriageways, this area was a large expanse of woodland and fields, with at least a dozen exits. The search proved fruitless. In the meantime, Marjory was taken to the police station for an examination and statement. She was eventually driven home at 5am, at which point her parents were informed.

The newspapers were quick to react and covered the story in great detail in the following day's editions. Marjory was interviewed and openly quoted by the press; but was able to add little to her original description of her assailant given to the police, that the man was probably about 5' 5" in height, around 30, and with a reddish complexion.

Perth was in a state of shock and paranoia as the city awoke to the news of the horrific attack and murder. The Buckie Braes were cordoned off from the public, to protect the crime scene from macabre souvenir hunters, and a huge search operation was then organised. Police constables and newspapers warned the public to be vigilant, and a watch was maintained on Perth railway and bus stations. Housewives locked their doors and men glanced nervously in every alleyway, vennel and dark corner. Three 'suspicious looking' men were arrested and shown to Marjory Fenwick, in a hastily organised identification parade, however she did not recognise them, and all were subsequently released. The police search of the Cuddies' Strip did not yield the murder weapon, and the officers' efforts were expanded to nearby fields and woodlands.

Heavy rain on Friday 17th and Saturday 18th August thwarted police efforts to use bloodhounds, in the hope a scent and trail might be picked up. The dogs proved ineffective, and speculation grew that the murderer had fled Perth and may be hiding elsewhere in Scotland. However, this assumption simply led to a widening of the hysteria and a dilution of police resources, as they were forced to follow up frantic calls from the public from all across the country. One vagrant was detained, then released, at Bridge of Allan; another at Perth General railway station. A man attempting to sell a shotgun at a pawnbrokers in Dundee was chased, as he fled the shop, but subsequently released after questioning. Lanarkshire and Glasgow City Police searched woodland in the vicinity of Muirhead, near Glasgow, for a tramp who had a attacked a local man with a cut-throat razor, however they were unable to trace him. In Crieff a 'rough looking man' seen bathing in the River Earn was apprehended, but also released. Calls came from as far away as Aberdeenshire, Dunfermline, and Ross-shire, but all turned out to be red herrings.

The funeral of Danny Kerrigan on 19th August, saw thousands line the streets of Perth, as the hearse made its way to Wellshill Cemetery. Plain clothed police officers lined the route in the hope of catching the murderer. However, their efforts were soon diverted when they were forced to lock the gates to the cemetery, to prevent thousands of members of the public from forcing their way into the proceedings. Following the service, a guard was placed on watch around the graveside. Partly to prevent ghoulish souvenir hunters, and partly in the hope that the murderer might visit the site in a fit of remorse.

On 21st August, a 1916 German army rifle was found in the police search of a nearby field. However, forensic tests of the body had established that the fatal wounds had been caused by a shotgun, not a revolver or rifle, as had first been thought. Police searches of the crime scene unearthed little else, except part of Marjory's necklace, which had been torn from her neck, and two spent shotgun cartridges. Neither the murder weapon, nor any of Marjory's clothing was ever found. Perth police were again forced to divert resources, following up scores of calls from the public who reported piles of discarded clothing in various locations in Perth and surrounding areas. All proved to be fruitless.

A full week after the murder, on 23rd August, a member of the public reported a fire burning in a field, close to the murder scene. The police rushed to the spot, in the hope that the killer may have been trying to destroy some vital evidence, but, once again, the incident proved to be a false trail. A passer-by had simply been careless with a cigarette butt.

No further forward with the investigation, and with

mounting pressure from the public, officers from Glasgow CID were drafted in to assist. Friday 24th August saw the arrival at Perth police station of Detective Lieutenant Leith and Detective Sergeant McDougall, from Glasgow. The officers were highly experienced and had both dealt with scores of murder cases. Their presence would see a shift in emphasis for the investigation and eventually a breakthrough. Detective Lieutenant Leith's first responsibility was to respond to a strange letter received by Marjory Fenwick, that morning. The note to Marjory had arrived by first post, was handwritten in block capitals – in an effort to disguise the handwriting – and bore a Dundee postmark:

> MEET ME AT PERTH GENERAL STATION 6.30 SATURDAY NIGHT, DUNDEE PLATFORM. REFUSE, THEN YOU'LL KNOW
>
> MAN IN BLUE

The letter was publicised in the local newspapers and hundreds of people assembled on the platforms and footbridge at Perth Station on Saturday evening, hoping to catch a glimpse of the killer, and play their part in a melodrama that seemed like a homespun version of *The 39 Steps* or *Shanghai Express*, both popular films that had recently screened at the Playhouse. Plain clothed police officers also mingled among the hundreds of people lining the station platforms, but all to no avail. If the writer of the letter had actually been at the railway station intending to meet Marjory, he would certainly have been frightened away by the mass, expectant crowd.

Coincidentally, a man in a blue suit had been witnessed on the day of the murder, in the field close to the where the shooting took place. Was he the enigmatic 'Man in Blue'?

The strange letter, and new evidence from a witness who had come forward on the same day, convinced the police that the murderer was still at large in Perth, and had not fled elsewhere. Perhaps, the police speculated, the man was a jilted former lover of Marjory's, hellbent on revenge?

William Pickard, a resident of Queen Street in Perth, had seen a man running past his house, in the direction of the city, at approximately 11pm on the night of murder. The timings and the description of the man matched those given by Marjory Fenwick. This convinced the detectives that the man must be local, with knowledge of the area, and would, more than likely, still be in the vicinity. Leads from further afield were now to be ignored and efforts to find the killer were redoubled within Perth itself.

Another witness came forward and remembered seeing a man on the morning of the murder, hiding among the bushes and the long grass, with an object held up close to his face. At first the witness thought it was a gun but, as he approached, he realised it was a large telescope. The witness spoke to the man, and they chatted about hunting and shooting rabbits. Three other witnesses, including two men working at a nearby farm, also reported hearing gunshots on the night of 15th August. They distinctly remembered hearing two shots, followed by a pause, then a third shot. It was common to hear poachers shooting rabbits, and they thought little of it at the time. However, their evidence seemed to match Marjory Fenwick's recollection of the events.

The detectives were now certain that a man who knew exactly where to hide and where to poach rabbits must surely be local.

The evidence regarding the telescope was unusual and piqued the interest of the detectives. How did this man obtain such an unlikely accessory? This would prove to be a hugely significant moment in the case. Another police officer then recalled the report of a burglary, which had been filed just a week or so earlier. The file was quickly sent for.

Staff at nearby Aberdalgie House, owned by Lady Laura Douglas, had reported a break in at the laundry adjoining the main building. Among the items stolen were a large telescope and handkerchief. Fingerprints had been obtained at the scene, from a casement window, which could be matched to a suspect, if one was found. Detectives now knew they were closing in on their man.

Enquiries continued in Perth until 29th August, a full two weeks since the murder, when a witness came forward stating that he had spotted a man living rough in a field, close to the scene of the murder. Detectives and several officers were despatched to the scene, they entered the man's tent and arrested him. Detective Leith immediately realised he was on the right track. The tent contained several of the items that had been reported stolen from Aberdalgie House. In addition, the man closely matched the description, given by Marjory Fenwick, of her assailant.

Asked his name, he replied, in a thick Irish accent, 'John McGuigan'.

An identification parade was organised at Perth Police Station. McGuigan was given the opportunity to choose his own place in the line, and Marjory was brought into the yard by Detective Leith. She then walked along the line and was asked to point out the man who had attacked her. As she passed McGuigan, according to one of the officers present, 'she gave a start – a sort of jump'.

She turned to Detective Leith and asked him, 'what should I do now'?

'Have you identified any person?' he responded.

'I am nearly certain', Marjory replied.

She looked again and added, 'Yes, I am positive'.

She was then asked to take a step forward and point to

the man. Doing so, she raised her finger and pointed to McGuigan. He looked her in the eye and said, 'You have made a mistake. I must resemble a man.'

McGuigan was led away to be charged by the Superintendent. He protested loudly as he was removed, 'I know there is a mistake somewhere. There must be. I must resemble a man or something'.

John McGuigan (who also used the alias John Milligan) was charged with four offences:

1. The murder of Daniel Kerrigan

2. The assault and rape of Marjory Fenwick

3. The burglary of the laundry at Aberdalgie House

4. The theft of Daniel Kerrigan's pocket-book containing 12 shillings

A court date was set for November at the High Court of Justiciary in Edinburgh. Lord Charles Aitchinson KC, the Lord Justice-Clerk would preside. A former brilliant defence counsel, MP, and champion of the underdog, Aitchinson had famously assisted Sir Arthur Conan Doyle in helping to secure the release of Oscar Slater (Scotland's most infamous miscarriage of justice) in 1929. Aitchinson had delivered a speech lasting 14 hours at Oscar Slater's appeal. He seemed the perfect choice to ensure balance and a fair trial, among the hysteria surrounding the case.

Public interest in the case remained unabated as the trial began on Monday 25th November 1935. Large crowds gathered outside the court, with many being refused entry. A female member of the jury fainted and was attended to by one of the medical witnesses in the case, Dr Anderson.

An excellent and robust defence was presented to the court by John Wardlaw Burnet KC, who would later become Sheriff of Fife, Kinross, and Edinburgh. The chief concern to the defence was the lack of witnesses to both the killing and the assault. Without the murder weapon, only circumstantial evidence linked McGuigan to the shooting. No witnesses could be found to corroborate Marjory Fenwick's story. Burnet questioned Marjory's recollection of the events – particularly her position when the fatal shot was fired, her version of the assault, and the police fingerprint evidence. Ballistic and forensic indications did seem to match Marjory's memory of the events. The first and second shots were fired from 10 - 15 yards away, and the third shot from probably closer than eight yards. Wadding from the shot cartridge was found close to the body. Following discharge of a shotgun, wadding normally travels no more than a maximum of eight yards, so the killer was certainly close when the third shot was fired.

Despite a strong questioning of the medical evidence by Burnet, the doctor's examination of Marjory Fenwick revealed bruising and marks to her neck, consistent with her claim that she was grabbed around the neck from behind. Other than minor bruises and abrasions, she had suffered no further external injuries.

The handkerchief used to bind her wrists, however, would prove to be probably the single most important piece of evidence in the trial. When Marjory managed to free herself and run for help, the handkerchief was still tied to her right wrist. It proved to carry a distinctive laundry mark, which matched the laundry mark found on other items at Aberdalgie House. This, together with the fingerprint evidence recovered from a casement window at the property and the items found in McGuigan's tent tied him directly to the robbery and to the assault on Marjory Fenwick. The police had taken great care to match the fingerprints, entirely removing the casement window and frame from the laundry at Aberdalgie House and sending it to their laboratory in Glasgow for special forensic examination. Marjory Fenwick's mother was shown the only items of her daughter's clothing recovered from the scene (her swagger coat, part of her necklace, and her suspender belt), which she identified as belonging to Marjory.

However, Wardlaw Burnet KC was not to be deterred, and summed up McGuigan's defence at great length and with much passion, expertise, and more than a little guile. To throw doubt on Marjory Fenwick's version of events, he firstly noted that she was extremely lucky not to have been hit by a stream of shotgun pellets, if her memory of the events was correct regarding her position at the time of the shooting. Her previous sexual activity was also questioned, which should have had no bearing on the case whatsoever; but did sow a seed of doubt in the jurors' minds. What was her true character? Was the murder an act of vengeance from a former lover?

There had also been poaching reported in the fields next to Buckie Braes, so the question of the shots having come from another poacher was also raised.

The external injuries to Marjory were superficial and, as attested to by the examining doctor, there was no reddening of her wrists, despite her claim that a handkerchief had bound her wrists together. The handkerchief was also produced in court to demonstrate the difficultly in securing two wrists together with it.

Cleverly, Burnet also reminded the jury that they sat in the very same courtroom where Scotland's greatest miscarriage of justice had taken place 26 years earlier – the conviction for murder of Oscar Slater.

Perhaps the most crucial point for the defence was the complete lack of other witnesses. The entire case rested on the solitary evidence of Marjory Fenwick, who had just undergone a traumatic ordeal, in near darkness. Could the death penalty really be imposed without a single other corroborating witness? Burnet urged the jury to consider only verdicts of not guilty or the particular Scottish verdict of not proven.

Lord Aitchinson was also troubled by this point and his summary of the case, directed at the jury, took more than two hours. He spoke of the gravity of their situation regarding their decision in a case that relied on just one witness, especially with evidence as 'flimsy' as a handkerchief. He also brought their attention to the importance of the stolen items linking the break in at Aberdalgie House to the assault on Marjory Fenwick, and thus to the shooting of Daniel Kerrigan.

The jury retired to consider their verdict. It was now the afternoon of Saturday 30th November 1935.

Finally, after two hours and twelve minutes, the jury returned.

'What is your verdict?', asked the Clerk of the Court, Mr Alexander Rae. The packed courtroom sat hushed in anticipation.

'Guilty', came the answer.

McGuigan was found unanimously guilty of the charge of housebreaking and of the assault on Marjory Fenwick. However, on the charge of the murder of Daniel Kerrigan the jury returned the verdict of not proven. The court was stunned into silence. This notoriously unsatisfactory Scottish verdict offers juries the chance to avoid choosing the ultimate sanction – and it was often taken.

In passing sentence, Lord Aitchinson revealed to the court McGuigan's previous convictions (they are not made available to the jury beforehand, to ensure each case is only heard on its own merits, and not coloured by the jury's opinion of the accused's past record). In 1929 McGuigan had been convicted of another assault, also of theft and housebreaking. Again in 1932 he was convicted of housebreaking, and a further charge followed in February 1934.

Lord Aitchinson told the court McGuigan was a dangerous criminal who deserved to be kept away from the public. He was sentenced to 10 years penal servitude and removed from the courtroom and taken to Peterhead Prison to begin his sentence.

Marjory Fenwick was given the news of McGuigan's sentence at home with her family, where she had returned to recuperate, following the ordeal of giving evidence. She was able to rebuild her life, later marrying in 1940 at St Columba's Church in Perth.

The parents of John McGuigan, also homeless, moved into the tent in which their son had been living. They were informed of the verdict while staying there. Later, in 1936, they moved to the Peterhead area, to be closer to their son, after he was assaulted and badly injured in a fight, while working at the prison quarry. It seems, in that strange sense of perverted justice that exists in prison, his fellow inmates exacted a brand of retribution that the court system could not.

John McGuigan returned to Ireland following his release.

The official verdict of not proven means the murder of Danny Kerrigan remains technically unsolved, although the police never looked for anyone else in relation to the incident.

FIVE SHOTS, TWO MURDERS, ONE SUICIDE

A casual labourer, Duncan Doig, aged 40, earned his living picking up odd jobs on the farms nestled in the rolling countryside around Perth. It was 1942, and the tide of the war had not yet turned in favour of the Allies. Further rationing restrictions had just been introduced to an already weary population, and news was slowly reaching Britain of the Japanese Navy's attacks on Ceylon, sinking Royal Navy battleships. The war still raged against Nazi Germany in the skies over Europe, and in North Africa too. Many men were abroad fighting in North Africa or the Far East.

Duncan Doig remained at home, however. His occupation was considered vital to the war effort, under the Government's Reserved Occupation Scheme; meaning he would not be called up to fight. Consequently, he was seen by many locals as a shirker, not prepared to 'do his bit'. With a temper easily inflamed – especially by alcohol - he frequently argued with fellow drinkers in the inns of Perth, when questioned about his patriotism to the cause and even his ancestry. Doig did come from a respectable and proud Scottish family, nevertheless, his father having been employed as a coachman at Lowfield in Luncarty.

Despite his temper, and the provocation of others testing his patriotism, Doig had never been in trouble with the police before. That would all change on the night of 4th May 1942.

Duncan Doig had rented the ground floor flat at number 3a Ruthven Avenue, a two-storey tenement in Perth, in the spring of 1941. Later that year he had met Elizabeth Ryan, a 42-year-old divorcee. Elizabeth, flame-haired and green-eyed, was originally from the Republic of Ireland. She had left her 20-year-old daughter Nancy at a convent school in Ireland and travelled to Scotland in 1939, taking work planting potatoes on the farms around the Fair City. After meeting while working together, Duncan Doig and Elizabeth started a relationship, and it was not long before Elizabeth moved into Doig's lodgings in Ruthven Avenue. Although Doig was sometimes sullen, the couple were mostly happy together despite the war, the perennial problem of money, and the accusing looks often directed at Doig by those who questioned his courage. That was soon to change, however.

Elizabeth informed Doig that her daughter, Nancy, would soon be travelling across from Ireland to live with them. Nancy had left the convent school and her mother had managed to find her employment on a potato farm close by. Elizabeth had already informed Nancy that they had a spare room in their house at Ruthven Avenue, and that her partner would not mind at all. Doig seemed annoyed at not being consulted – particularly as the property was his - but quickly realised he had little choice in the matter.

Virtually from the outset, the arrival of Nancy from Ireland seemed to place a huge strain on the relationship between Doig and Elizabeth, and on the household generally. The couple frequently argued, often resulting in Elizabeth forcing Doig to leave the house. Nancy, of course, always took her mother's side. Doig would return days later, often drunk and frequently in the blackest of moods, demanding to be let into his own house. The quarrels were loud, and a series of complaints were lodged by their neighbours at the Perth City police station.

Finally, around March 1942, the worsening situation appears to have become too much for the conflicted Duncan Doig to bear. He moved out of the house and, instead, found himself new lodgings in a small and dingy terraced house in the narrow and dark confines of Low Street in Perth. Yet, surprisingly, in an act of kindness, rather than seeing Elizabeth and Nancy forced out of Ruthven Avenue, Doig signed over the tenancy and all his furniture to his ex-partner and her daughter. Whether they managed to persuade him to do so, or whether it was an unexpected act of generosity on Doig's part is not known. It was definitely not an act consistent with his usual behaviour. Nevertheless, it was certainly an extremely charitable, if uncharacteristic, one. Perhaps Doig had hoped that he would be able to resurrect his relationship with Elizabeth through his act of kindness. However, his gesture brought with it an unfortunate side effect which Doig almost certainly had not realised at the time. Now, without the prior permission of Elizabeth, his presence at Ruthven Avenue would be legally regarded as an act of trespass. Although he attempted to visit Elizabeth on several occasions during March and April of 1942, she invariably refused him entry. Again, this resulted in furious arguments between the couple. Doig threatened to force his way inside on several occasions and, in return, Elizabeth retaliated by shouting for the local police constable and threatening to have Doig arrested. Each time this occurred Doig was forced to leave again, and trudge back to his lonely dwellings in Low Street, an angry, humiliated, and frustrated man.

Unfortunately, the solitude of his lodgings failed to calm Doig's anger. Instead, the desire for vengeance grew stronger inside him. While drowning his sorrows in the public houses of Perth, he openly swore revenge on his former lover and her daughter, before once again returning alone to his dwellings in Low Street, lonely, smarting, and smouldering. His neighbours would later claim that they too often heard overheard Doig muttering drunken threats towards his former lover Elizabeth.

At some time on the morning of Sunday 3rd May 1942, Doig borrowed a double-barrelled shotgun from a fellow worker at the farm where he had been employed during the previous month, claiming he needed the gun to shoot pigeons with (a practice which was frowned upon during the war, but which was continued regardless).

Now, brooding alone in his lodgings and clutching the shotgun tightly, he waited for nightfall and for the streets to become silent as the population of the city pulled down their blackout blinds and retired for the night. The blackout ensured that the streets would be pitch black, with only the light from the moon to reveal his identity to any passers-by. Finally, in the small hours of Monday 4th May, Doig loaded the magazine and the chamber of the shotgun with five cartridges, carefully placing a further five cartridges, within easy reach, in the pocket of his jacket. He then ventured out onto the dark street and walked quickly past the terraced cottages of the city. Doig was not spotted by any potential witness, who may have been able to prevent him, or perhaps telephone the police. Every house had its windows obscured by the required blackout blinds and crisscrossed blast tape. With the blackout still in force in 1942, no streetlights blazing, and little traffic on the deserted streets, it would have been relatively easy for the shadowy figure of Doig to conceal the shotgun under the folds of his jacket. With just the light from a three-quarter moon partially hidden by cloud, he headed north, turning along Crieff Road towards Ruthven Avenue.

It was close to 3am when he eventually reached his former dwelling. It was deathly quiet and, in order to affect an entry, Doig crept silently along the side of the building, climbed over the back wall, and stepped down silently into the back yard. Taking care to avoid the drying lines and the metal dustbins, he carefully removed his right shoe. Placing his right hand inside the shoe he used it to shatter the pane of the ground floor bathroom window and climbed inside, crunching broken glass as he did. Hoping that the noise of the smashed glass had not woken the occupants, he removed his left shoe and tiptoed silently along the corridor in his socks, carefully carrying his shoes.

Meanwhile, despite Doig's efforts to remain silent, Elizabeth's daughter Nancy had been woken by the sound of smashing glass. She sat up, her heart pounding, before jumping straight out of bed and running across the corridor into her mother's room. Shaking with terror, both women sat cowering on the bed. They instinctively knew that the alarming noise was not that of a normal burglar. In a moment of intense fear, they were both gripped with the ominous realisation that the sound was almost certainly that of Duncan Doig come to seek his terrible revenge on the women that he had condemned for ruining his life.

Doig entered the room silently – his large frame briefly illuminated in the door frame - and, rather than switch on the electric light, he carefully unscrewed the lightbulb and placed it on the floor next to his shoes. Whatever fate he had in store for Elizabeth and Nancy would take place in the dark of that small bedroom. We can only imagine the intense terror the two women must have felt as Doig produced the shotgun from under his jacket. In near darkness the horror of their situation rendered the two women speechless. Doig did not prolong their agony, however. He fired once at Nancy, hitting her in the chest, and killing her instantly. The force of the impact at such close range flung her body backwards in a heap. Within an instant of Doig firing the shotgun, as he turned to level the weapon at Elizabeth, she leapt quickly from the bed and, passing Doig, attempted to escape into the narrow passageway beyond the bedroom door. Doig turned and pursued her, shouting out her name, and firing the shotgun again and again. Elizabeth ran into her daughter's bedroom and vainly attempted to turn the stiff catch and escape through the window, which opened out at ground level onto the road outside. As she frantically tried to pull the window frame open, Doig fired again, and the shotgun cartridge exploded into her body. The windowpane was shattered as the deafening blast from the shotgun rang out around the room and the street outside. Whether she had managed to break the glass or whether the force of the cartridge's impact had smashed her body against the windowpane is not known. Elizabeth slumped to the floor underneath the window. She did not die instantaneously but lay there for a short while until her troubled breathing ceased and she finally fell silent. Doig watched, motionless, in the half light.

In the meantime, the sound of shots had woken Mrs Ames, who occupied the upstairs flat, and she telephoned the Perth City Police. She would later tell the inquest that she 'heard the sound of a gunshot, then there was the sound of a woman screaming as she ran, with a man's voice shouting. Then there was another shot. Then five minutes silence, then a further shot.'

Meanwhile, the room became silent as Elizabeth Ryan drew her terminal breath, Doig sat down on the end of the bed. He placed the remaining five cartridges on the bedroom floor and, carefully placing the shotgun under his chin, pulled the trigger.

Constables McCartney and Gustavson were first on the scene. When they entered the bedroom, they realised that Doig was still alive and quickly telephoned for an ambulance. However, he had horrific wounds to his face and head and was pronounced dead on arrival at Perth Royal Infirmary.

Both Elizabeth and Nancy were buried in the same grave at Wellshill Cemetery in Perth five days later. A Roman Catholic priest carried out the ceremony, as had always been Elizabeth's wish. The only mourner was Elizabeth's brother Michael, who Perth Police had managed to trace to South Wales, where he had taken employment in the mining industry.

The scene of the tragic double murder was, perhaps fittingly, demolished when Ruthven Avenue was redeveloped during the 1960s and 1970s. The exact location of the shocking events on that infamous night lie somewhere underneath what is now Fairfield Avenue. Perhaps it is appropriate that the precise whereabouts of this shocking crime are now gone forever.

Douglas Doig's body was taken from Perth Royal Infirmary and buried, without ceremony, in an unmarked grave. It was rumoured that his body was buried alongside a piece of paper containing the quotation usually associated with the Chinese philosopher Confucius:

> *Before you embark on a journey of revenge,*
> *first dig two graves.*

THE MEGGERNIE MURDER

The Rev EJ Simmons and his good friend Mr Beaumont Featherstone visited Meggernie Castle, at Glen Lyon, in Perthshire during August 1870 to enjoy some shooting and fishing (a popular pastime among the gentry and well-off middle classes during the Victorian era).

Meggernie Castle is a whitewashed and imposing sixteenth-century tower house and mansion, built in the traditional Scottish style. The castle is located in the 'longest, loneliest and loveliest glen in Scotland' (as described by Sir Walter Scott), to the north of Loch Tay in Highland Perthshire.

In 1870 the castle was owned by a Mr Herbert Wood, a friend of Beaumont Featherstone, and he frequently invited guests to share his hospitality. Prior to their visit, neither the Rev. Simmons nor Mr Featherstone had heard any stories of a sinister nature regarding the castle and were looking forward to a tranquil and enjoyable stay in the Scottish countryside. Yet the circumstances of their weekend would prove to be anything other than peaceful or pleasurable. Indeed, their experience was so traumatic it would be several years before either could openly discuss the happenings of that weekend.

On their arrival at Meggernie each man was housed in one of the large bedrooms located in the original tower, as the rest of the accommodation in the castle was already occupied. While hanging his hunting attire away Beaumont Featherstone noticed a small connecting door located at the back of the closet, which seemed to join the two rooms. However, the door appeared to be steadfastly sealed and could not be opened. It appeared to have remained untouched for many years. Both men assumed that the two rooms had been interconnected at some point in the past; and thought little more of the matter.

Following a busy and tiring day and a hearty supper the men retired to their respective rooms in the tower. Rev Simmons seemed to have been very pleased with his room, which enjoyed splendid views to the north and the south, across the parkland and to the mountains beyond. He did not bother to light the oil lamp by his bedside, just a candle that had been thoughtfully provided.

He fell asleep quickly, accompanied by the flickering flame from the candle, which he had placed close by on his nightstand. Suddenly, around 2am in the morning he was woken by a strange sensation. A curious burning or scorching feeling on his right cheek felt so intense that he sat bolt upright. He instinctively put his hand up to his face, thinking that he turned over in his sleep and somehow knocked over the candle, which was still burning on the nightstand beside his bed. Yet the candle had remained unmoved. It was still burning, and dimly lit the room around him. It was pitch black outside.

Yet the sensation from the pain was acutely real. It had seemed to pass right through to his cheekbone, although, bizarrely, the pressure on his flesh had initially felt light, like a gentle kiss. Then he witnessed something in the half-light of the bedroom that chilled him to the bones.

He wrote a letter several years later, in which he explained exactly what he had experienced:

I was awakened in the night by what appeared to be a burning kiss, it appeared to scorch the flesh through to the cheek bone. I jumped up in bed and distinctly saw the upper half body of a Lady pass from the side of my bed, go along the room and through the door that was screwed up tight, as if going into Beaumont's room.

Simmons jumped up, lit the lamp by his bedside, and at once tried the door at the back of the closet, that he had noticed earlier, and that had previously linked the two bedrooms. However, it had been locked and screwed into the frame, and could not be opened, even with a considerable amount of force. He then gingerly checked his cheek, expecting to find it blistered from the hot kiss, but there was no mark, although it ached, just as if it had been burnt. Although in a state of shock, Simmons did not knock on his friend's bedroom door or awaken any other members of the household. Instead, he took the lamp in his hand and ventured onto the stairs outside his room in search of the mysterious apparition. He nervously ventured along the corridor, holding the oil lamp in front of him to illuminate the shadowy corners. However, he could find no evidence of any disturbance, or see anything that would account for what he had experienced. He returned, anxious and weary, to his bed. There was a chill in the air; and he spent the reminder of the night troubled as he nervously awaited the morning light.

With the welcome advent of morning, Simmons knocked on the door of his friend who appeared at once in the doorway, looking shocked, gaunt and shaking. Beaumont Featherstone had also suffered a similar experience during the night. At about 2.30am he too had seen the 'floating torso' (as he described it) of a beautiful woman, but one with a look of grim despair etched across her bloody face. She had appeared through the locked door adjoining the rooms and then disappeared again. He recounted to his friend, Rev Simmons, that he had first been woken by an eerie pink light in the room, and then noticed a pale lady standing at the foot of his bed. His first thought, in the dim light, was that it must have been the housekeeper, as the doors to the bedrooms from the landing were not locked. However, as he started to wake fully, he realised it was the floating torso of a young woman. The apparition slowly glided along the side of his bed and leaned over him, as he remained terrified and motionless. Although this lasted only a matter of seconds, it felt like hours.

His only thought was to run into the corridor. He slowly plucked up the courage to move but, when he sat up, the ghostly figure of the woman retreated noiselessly and quickly into the closet or cupboard that connected with the room occupied by Simmons. Stiffening his resolve, Featherstone struck a light and followed the vision towards the tiny closet; however, it was empty apart from a towel rail on the wall. At the back of the closet the door adjoining the two rooms was steadfastly shut and the closet offered no other hiding place. Looking around the room, even under the bed, he could find nothing; and he too then spent an uncomfortable and fraught night sleeping fitfully and shaking in fear.

The following morning both men quickly compared notes, and both agreed the apparition was the floating torso of a beautiful young woman, who appeared in great distress. At breakfast, Simmons was keen to tell the story to the other guests. However (he later recalled), 'a look from Mrs Herbert Wood stopped me, for she was afraid it would alarm her other guests'.

The two men diplomatically waited for the other guests to disperse after breakfast before reporting their nocturnal experience to their hosts. After hearing their tale, Herbert Wood nodded knowingly, before describing in detail the story of a previous female guest who had disturbed the whole household by wakening everybody in the middle of the night complaining that she had felt the sensation of a woman lying down beside her. In another separate incident a servant girl, who had been working in the castle's kitchen, reported seeing the lower half of a woman's body floating silently along the stone passage. She had fled in terror. This sighting perplexed everyone, as previous witnesses only recalled seeing the floating upper part of a woman's body.

It transpired, in fact, that most of the servants refused to even work in the old part of the house – much to the annoyance of Herbert Wood (although this might explain why he was anxious that the matter was not brought up at the breakfast table). It was also said that a similar apparition had been seen several times, covered in blood, either beside the avenue of lime trees in the castle's parkland or close by in the local graveyard.

Beaumont Featherstone left the castle quite soon afterwards, clearly traumatised by his experience. However Simmons stayed on for several more days, although he refused to sleep in the same bedroom again.

However, about ten days later, while Simmons was sitting writing a letter at the desk in the castle's drawing-room, the heavy, iron-studded oak door suddenly opened, although nobody appeared to be on the other side. The room suddenly, and inexplicably, became icy cold. As he looked up from his writing, the ghostly half-figure of the same woman glided noiselessly past him. Later that night, as he walked along one of the passageways, he had another ghostly encounter when he came across the same apparition of the distressed young woman, looking at him through an outside window. He knew instantly, it was the same beautiful yet anguished lady that he had encountered previously. His interest had been aroused and he became determined to research the sinister happenings at Meggernie Castle. However, his initial attempts to interview neighbours, and amongst the local community, met with little success. There was a reluctance to discuss the matter or repeat old stories to strangers:

The people seemed to dislike talking on the subject extensively and looked angered when questioned about it, he would later write in his notes.

Despite this obstacle, Simmons undertook some historical research and was able to suggest that the origins of the sightings may have been related to a legend regarding one of the Menzies lairds of Meggernie, who had murdered his young wife in a fit of jealous rage.

Meggernie was originally one of several strongholds built by Colin Campbell of Glen Lyon, one of the branches of the powerful Campbell clan. In later years the property passed on to the Menzies of Culdares, and the murderous legend that Simmons unearthed related to one of this family. Around the year 1750, one of the Menzies lairds, had married a beautiful young bride, many years younger than he was. Although there were no tales, or rumours, of infidelity by his young bride, Menzies felt unable to trust her. His jealousy grew to such an extent that he refused to believe any reassurances she gave him. If she ever tried to placate him he would, instead, interpret her actions as suspicious and assume she was attempting to conceal a guilty secret. Finally, he snapped and – in a furious and jealous rage – sought his revenge on his unfaithful wife, and fatally attacked her.

In a rushed and desperate attempt to conceal the deed, and escape any punishment, Menzies hacked her bloody corpse into two pieces and hid the remains, secured in a chest, and locked in a closet in one of the rooms in the tower. This room later became known as the 'haunted room'. Menzies then informed his staff and neighbours that his wife had gone away on a visit to relatives; and that he then intended to join her shortly. His staff were led to believe that their master and his young wife would be making a long trip to the continent and would be away for some time. It was commonplace at that time for the wealthy to visit the historic sites of Europe, and the trip would not have aroused suspicion. Consequently, the castle was shut up and it was several months before the Menzies Laird returned, bringing with him the sad news that his wife had drowned in an Italian lake during their visit to Europe.

It appears that Menzies then removed his wife's decaying remains from the chest in the closet and attempted to dispose of them. This surely must have been an unpleasant task in the extreme, and doubtlessly affected him for the remainder of his life

He buried the bottom half of his wife's body in the family graveyard, intending to dispose of the upper half of her body the next day. However, Menzies died suddenly before he was able to move the remains of her torso. Whether his death was natural, accidental, or by the hand of someone who had guessed the awful truth, is not known. He was found dead the following morning in the tower; some suggest that he may have died of a heart attack after the exertions of moving the corpse. Others that he may have fallen. Rumours also spread that he was slain by his wife's suspicious relatives, or that he may have been frightened to death by the apparition of his murdered wife.

From this point onwards, many more visitors reported seeing strange manifestations at the castle. Each story was remarkable in its similarity to the sightings recorded by Mr Featherstone and Rev Simmons. In fact, many years later, Beaumont Featherstone met a woman in a hotel who had undergone the exact same experience as he had. The apparition always had two parts: the top half of a woman, often seen in the upper rooms in the tower and the lower half of a body, wearing a blood-splattered dress, seen on the ground floor, or sometimes outside in the castle grounds, or nearby in the family graveyard.

Colonel Kinloch Grant and his wife, who had been staying at the castle around the year 1900, reported waking in the night to see the apparition of a woman bending over them. Grant was Her Majesty's Inspector of Constabulary, and not prone to flights of fancy.

In 1928 Dr Douglas MacKay from Aberfeldy made a house call at Meggernie Castle; and was compelled to stay the night, due to the late hour. He stayed in one of the lower rooms in the old tower and claimed to have heard footsteps outside his room during the night. He had the strong impression that someone had entered the room, although the door had not been opened. He sat up in his bed and clearly saw the upper part of the apparition floating along the wall, near the ceiling. It emitted an eerie pink glow, similar to that reported by Mr Featherstone. Within seconds it was gone. Many years later, in 1958, the writer Alasdair MacGregor contacted Dr MacKay to discuss the story. Even 30 years later the doctor did not waiver from his belief that he had witnessed a ghost, and claimed it was the most vivid and extraordinary event he had ever experienced.

To add some credence to the story, during renovation work on the castle around 1910, the upper bones of a skeleton were discovered beneath the floor in one of the upper chambers. The remains were buried; however, hauntings and manifestations continued to be reported, including banging and knockings. It was often reported that a sharp rapping sound heralded an appearance of the dismembered ghost.

So, did Rev Simmons and Mr Beaumont Featherstone concoct the story and had they, in fact, already heard previous stories of the ghost at Meggernie Castle (despite both claiming they had no previous knowledge)? If they did, they certainly never sought any gain, financial or otherwise. Indeed, it was many years – 12 to be exact – before either one publicly mentioned the events of 1870. Beaumont Featherstone, it seems, did not even like to mention the sighting for fear of ridicule, so it seems unlikely either would have concocted such a story.

Beaumont Featherstone, even wrote the following in one his last letters prior to his death:

I don't care to talk to anyone about it, and I hate writing about it and never have before, as I don't like being laughed at for the reason that it was not tosh.

THE FORGOTTEN KILLINGS

December 1918. The armistice to end the Great War had been signed just one month earlier. The demobilisation of Scotland's battle-weary troops was slowly beginning, as families in Perthshire began to prepare to welcome home their sons, husbands and fathers.

Tragically, for many, their wait would be much longer. Nervous families still waited anxiously at homes for news of the forgotten soldiers, those that had been captured and incarcerated in German prisoner of war camps. Access to any information was difficult to obtain and agonisingly slow to reach home. Families waited impatiently for a letter, a telegram, or perhaps a surprise knock at the door, informing them that their son was alive and well and would be repatriated soon.

For one Perth family, however, the news they received on Monday December 9th, 1918, came, not as a relief, but as a confirmation of their worst fears. Mr Peter Baxter and his wife resided in James Street, Perth. Their son James, a former pupil of Perth Academy, had been reported missing in late March 1918, during the last big German offensive.

It would be almost nine long months until they received any further news. Finally, in early December, a letter arrived from a comrade-in-arms of their son, rather than via any official source. The letter came from a Private Jim Stewart, who himself had just returned from Freiburg prisoner of war camp in Germany, to his family home in St Ann's Lane, Perth. According to Private Stewart, the Baxter's son James had been murdered by a guard at the camp. In an act of terrible retribution, a guard had killed their son because he had failed to hear a command given to him. Unknown to the German guard, James Baxter suffered from a damaged cardrum which had led to deafness in one ear. Prior to signing up he had frequently attended the doctor in Perth. It seemed that James had failed to hear an instruction given to him by the guard.

The full story of the murder of Private James Baxter would come one week later, when his parents received a letter from another soldier who had returned from Germany and had secretly witnessed the murder. His name was Private Fred Bungay of the North Staffordshire's, who had been a fellow prisoner alongside Baxter. The pair had become good friends and Private Bungay very much wanted to tell Mrs Baxter the full story of exactly what had happened to their son:

Dear Madam,

I will let you know all I can about your son as he was a very nice chap, and we all respected him. I was a prisoner myself captured on the 21st of March last, the same time as Mr Baxter. Your son came to our camp at Freiburg about two months after me, and this affair happened at the end of September. We were going to work, climbing a bank to pick bramble leaves (to make tea for the German guards) *and James walked in a different direction to the rest of us. The guard, a real bully, called out, but I think a cold caused deafness and James did not hear him. The guard then yelled out, and I think James might have been frightened, for he started to run. Poor chap, he was weak, suffering from want of food, I reckon, and he stumbled when he reached the bank. The guard went forward and beat him with the butt end of his rifle, and then shot him through the back. God! It was awful to be there and see a chum murdered in cold blood like that.*

I hid behind some bushes, and I was the only one to see the brutal attack on a defenceless man. The guard walked off to give the alarm and fetch the camp doctor. I rushed up and me and two pals moved him to a more comfortable position at the bottom of the bank, but he died soon after. I took out James's pocket-book for his address and found a photo of him with a child, but I had to put it back quickly when the guards came. The camp interpreter afterwards got the wallet. Three days later we buried him. I and my pals dug his grave at the cemetery in the village. When we buried him there was a German priest there and the rest of the boys. The Germans tried to take his ring off, but his finger was too swollen and it was buried with him (the ring had been given to James by his sweetheart Elsie when the couple had become engaged).

The affair was hushed up and I hear that the guard declared what he did was in self-defence, and that Baxter had tried to strangle him. It is a lie for he had his back to the guard. It would have been no good for me to interfere, for the guard would have shot me I believe.

If there is any more you would like to know about him let me know, and I will be only too pleased to tell you if I can. You have got my sympathy.

Yours sincerely

Fred Bungay (Private)

Private James Baxter 316963 had joined the Special Company of the Royal Engineers at Bedford in August 1917. (He had been away from Perth, working in Dunstable at the time). After his three months of initial training, he then proceeded to his unit in France. Baxter was captured in the German push of 21st March 1918, and had been a prisoner for almost nine months, firstly at Parchim, then Wesel POW Camp. His name is recorded on a memorial at Perth Academy, along with the many others who lost their lives during the Great War. His body was buried in the village cemetery at Steinen, in Alsace. James Baxter was just 31 years of age.

Also in December 1918, a pale and emaciated soldier returned at last to his family home in Moulin, near Pitlochry. A shadow of his former self, Private William

Grant had endured imprisonment in a POW camp longer than perhaps any other British soldier during the Great War.

Already an experienced soldier, even at the beginning of the Great War, he had served as a reservist during the Boer War (winning the South African Medal), William Grant had signed up on 4th August 1914 – the first day of the Great War. He enlisted in the Queen's Own Cameron Highlanders. After basic training at Edinburgh, his battalion mobilised for war and shipped to Le Havre. William Grant saw immediate action on the Western Front with the 1st Brigade of the 1st Division. His unit joined others as part of the British Expeditionary Force (BEF) fighting from Arras in France, to Nieuwpoort on the Belgian coast, from 10th October to mid-November 1914. The battle became known as the First Battle of Ypres, in which the BEF suffered casualties and losses amounting to a staggering 58,000 men.

On the first day of a skirmish with German troops at Langemarck on 19th October, William Grant was captured and held prisoner by the German division his unit had encountered. Incarcerated firstly in a collection of shell damaged buildings in the village, he was due to be taken to one of the newly built POW camps, at that moment being hastily erected further behind the German lines. However, a British raiding party managed to release him (and other captured Cameron Highlanders) under cover of darkness on the early morning of 21st October. During his brief imprisonment Grant had witnessed a supply dump of German rifles stored in a cellar. Before dashing for freedom with the rescue party, Grant stopped to damage the boxes of rifles, rendering them useless to the Germans.

As the sun rose on the morning of the 21st, William Grant was safely back with his unit. However, there was no pause for breath. An encounter with another German unit saw Grant captured again, just hours after being freed. This time there was to be no reprieve for Grant and his fellow Highlanders. More than 18,500 members of the BEF were captured during the battle. Grant and other Cameron Highlanders were marched away at gunpoint and herded onto a train destined for Göttingen Camp, situated on a hillside just outside the old university town of Göttingen. The men, who all wore kilts during battle, were easily identified as Scots. The German guards took great delight in sliding open the doors of the goods carriages as the train stopped at various stations en route for Göttingen. The locals then took great delight in jeering and shouting at the soldiers 'Schottländers, Schottländers', spitting on them, and throwing projectiles, before the doors were closed and the train rattled on again.

The camp at Göttingen became known as a 'Propaganda Camp', one used by the Germans as an international showcase to highlight its fair treatment of prisoners. Classes and lectures for the welfare of the prisoners were reportedly held at this camp by Professor Stange of Göttingen University. The Göttingen camp effectiveness as a propaganda tool for the Germans was achieved mainly as a result of Professor Stange's involvement. He began writing a book on the subject, almost immediately, entitled *Das Gefengenenlager in Göttingen* (The Prison Camp at

Göttingen) which was published in Germany during 1916.

According to the propaganda issued by the Germans, a YMCA Hall was built, prisoners were issued with money to spend at the camp shop, books and chess sets were issued. The POWs were often photographed in a series of staged pictures, showing them chatting or engaged in various healthy activities. The reality, however, was very different for William Grant and the other prisoners.

Life in camp was severe. Food was scarce and, what little sustenance did exist was unpalatable. Prisoners were forced to turn out and parade barefoot for a period of two hours, often in heavy snow or freezing rain. The men were organised into work parties and expected to perform gruelling work duties for the Germans. Often weak with hunger and fatigue this practice sapped all the men's' strength. On one occasion a prisoner complained of sickness, saying he would be unable to join the work party. He was shot dead by the guards in front of his fellow prisoners.

Unsanitary conditions caused a severe typhus epidemic to break out in 1915. This was partly countered with the installation of modern latrines, disinfection vats to remove lice from clothing, and shower or bath houses built for the prisoners.

Sickness was rife in Göttingen Camp; however, the men were punished if they declared themselves unfit to work. Following one such incident Private Grant and several other sick men were forced to stand to attention for five days against a stone wall. On another occasion they were made to sleep on the water covered floor of a freezing washhouse.

Every effort was made to break the prisoners mentally, too. On arriving at the camp in 1914 the guards taunted the prisoners, telling them that Britain was beaten. The men were deprived of news, relying on what the guards told them and on any morsels of information they could glean from new arrivals. Always starved of food, the men were kept alive by parcels arriving from home.

However, by the middle of 1918 the tide of the war had started to turn. News of a German plea for an armistice had filtered through. There were many Russian prisoners at the camp too, and when news of the revolution in their home country reached them, they were jubilant. By 8th November the prisoners were told they were to be set free. A group of revolutionaries among the Russian captives started a revolution of their own. Windows were smashed, the guards set upon and beaten, and the buttons ripped from their tunics, in a sustained campaign of revenge for their inhumane treatment.

This time there were reprisals from the German guards and much violence was inflicted on the prisoners.

However, when the armistice was eventually signed the men were finally set free. On 13th November William Grant and his fellow Highlanders were packed on a train bound for Holland, a ship to Scotland and finally back home. On arriving in Pitlochry, Private Grant, tired and emotional, told his family:

Many a time during the dark days of the war we were so weak that we said to each other "we will never see home again". But we would have died happy if we only saw our country on the winning side. And now the vision of home has come true, though I can hardly realise it yet.

There was understandable anger among the returning prisoners. Their desire for revenge and retribution against the guards, who had treated them so badly, was clear. 'Something must be done, and done now', Private Grant wrote.

As the stories emerged the demands for reprisals grew. At a meeting in Dundee the city's MP, Winston Churchill, was asked to act:

As Mr Churchill has, no doubt, observed from the articles which have appeared in the Dundee Advertiser *yesterday and today, an especially bad case of Hun brutality - having a fatal ending - took place towards the end of September, at Steinen Camp, Baden, in Alsace, to a Scottish Royal Engineer soldier. Does Mr Churchill not think such a case demands War Office inquiry to punish the Hun guard and give reparation to the relatives, and would he kindly move in the matter?*

It was noted in the record of the meeting that Mr Churchill answered 'Certainly'.

Despite Winston Churchill's, promise there were comparatively few prosecutions for war crimes pursued against German guards who had served at the various prison camps. There seems to be no record of any attempt to trace the killer of James Baxter, nor the man whose death was witnessed by William Grant. There seems to have been little appetite for uncovering yet more stories of death from the war. The sensitivities of the British people, it seems, were not ready for yet more horrors to be unearthed.

Meanwhile, and not always known by their families at home, the army had made its own preparations for the possibility that large numbers of men would be killed or reported missing. Before departing for France, each soldier had been asked to prepare a simple will. If they did not return from the conflict, their families would receive a War Office envelope containing their loved one's will. Such envelopes were received by the families of many of the men who had been interned in POW camps; and were assumed to be dead.

While those that died at the front were honoured, those missing were mourned, those killed in mysterious circumstances at POW camps seem to have been largely forgotten by the authorities.

The total number of men who died at German POW camps during the Great War is not known. Estimates range between 6 and 10% of the 1,000,000 men who were captured. It appears to be one of the least written about, and least discussed, parts of the conflict.

THE MAN WHO WAS HANGED TWICE

It was the beginning of September 1749, just four years after the Jacobite rising. Scotland was still an unruly place and did not have the benefit of a professional police force, like that which had been recently established in London. Around midday, a stray dog was witnessed running about in the streets of Muthill, a village four miles to the south of Crieff, in Perthshire. Nobody recognised the stray hound but, to the horror of the inhabitants, they noticed that the dog was carrying something in its mouth - the lower section of a human leg, with a stocking and a woman's shoe still on it.

Alarmed by this gruesome spectacle, the inhabitants of Muthill hastily organised a search, but despite a comprehensive hunt were unable to locate a body. The severed leg was showing signs of decomposition, so the villagers reached the natural conclusion that the victim had suffered this horrific injury some time ago and, in all probability, was unlikely to have survived. If someone had received medical attention for such an injury, it was improbable that the news would not have spread like wildfire around the community.

One of the villagers suggested using the dog to track the scent back to the victim. Everyone agreed and the animal was promptly tied up until it became hungry. Once released, the dog ran off in the direction from which it had first entered the village, presumably following the scent that had previously led it to the severed leg of the unknown victim. Several men from Muthill followed the dog into the grounds of Pitkellony House, behind the row of houses on the north side of the main street in the village. The large house and impressive estate were owned by David Drummond, of the Clan Drummond. There, in a secluded hollow under a copse of large trees in the west corner of the park, the party began searching in the area shown most interest in by the excited dog. First to be discovered was a human skull, followed by some partly decomposed garments of female clothing (now rotting and discoloured from the long period of time spent underground). About forty yards further to the west the group discovered part of a woman's backbone and, nearby, another human leg and thigh. The decomposing flesh on the bones had almost gone as a result of being constantly picked at by the birds and wild animals that populated the estate. The next horrific discovery was that of the woman's gown, a quantity of putrid flesh, a child's frock, and, scattered across the ground, part of the child's ribs and backbone, which had clearly been discarded by a scavenging animal.

The sight was a gruesome one and no time was lost in sending for the police constable in Crieff, Grigor Murray. Meanwhile, before darkness fell, a further search was made of the surrounding parkland. This search yielded several puzzling clues including a new reaping-hook, a small luggie (a pail or large dish), two women's shifts, a linen cap (known as a mutch), together with the remains of some bread and cheese. From this it was concluded that the woman may been on her way to the Lothians to shear sheep or help with the harvest (which was a common form of economic migration during that era). If the murdered woman had been travelling to work on the late summer harvest that seemed to indicate that she had set out probably no earlier than four or five weeks prior to the gruesome discovery of her body.

A group of local workers, who had happened to pass through the grounds at the end of July, recalled seeing a local man in the same spot. The man had been sitting, together with his wife and child, resting under the shade of the same large trees. They had recognised the man but had thought nothing more at the time. Fortunately, one of the group remembered the man's name, Alexander McCowan.

Alexander McCowan was known to still live in the area; however, he had told his neighbours and friends that his wife Alison and child had recently left for Edinburgh to work on a farm. No one had seen her since. Constable Grigor Murray was issued with a warrant for the arrest of Alexander McCowan, who was traced to a dwelling in Comrie, a village a few miles to the northwest. Constable Murray, together with an angry posse of locals, apprehended McCowan and publicly charged him with the murder of his wife and child. McCowan seemed unperturbed by his arrest; but was furious at being prevented from attending a dancing ball that evening, for which he had been in the middle of preparing!

McCowan was then tried at Perth Sheriff Court at the end of September 1749 for the murder of his wife Alison and their child. Despite appearing remarkably unconcerned during the trial, by the weight of circumstantial evidence against him, McCowan was found guilty and the judge immediately condemned him to death by hanging. However, after the sentence of death was passed by the judge, McCowan finally admitted his guilt and, at great length, made a full and eloquent confession to the packed courthouse, in a desperate plea of contrition and guilt.

Despite the sentence of death having already been passed, the Sheriff allowed McCowan to address the court (a highly unusual occurrence in 1749 when prisoners were not allowed to speak in their own defence). McCowan seized upon the opportunity and began to recount his story, addressing his comments to the throngs of spectators, rather than to the Sheriff. McCowan claimed that he was really a hero who had returned to the area two years earlier, in 1747, following a period in hiding in the aftermath of the Jacobite defeat at the Battle of Culloden. He had started a relationship with Alison at that time.

However, fearing Redcoat reprisals he had remained in hiding, moving from secret location to secret location for almost two years. McCowan informed the court, with all the passion he could muster, that in 1746 he had fought next to Bonnie Prince Charlie himself at Culloden, and at heart he was a loyal Scot. However, within a few weeks of commencing his courtship of Alison he became furious with her when she informed him that she was with child. In a furious fit of temper, McCowan enlisted as a soldier once again, this time with the British Redcoat Army, and left Alison to raise the child alone. He then travelled overseas to serve King George II. McCowan claimed to the court that, before departing, he had informed Alison, 'I might return one day, after the child is born, but I cannot promise such a thing!'

After more than a year away, both in England and abroad, he returned to that quiet corner of Perthshire; and it appears (outwardly at least) that he renewed a blissful relationship with Alison and the child. The reunited family moved into tiny lodgings together in Crieff. Before long, Alison became pregnant once again. Publicly, McCowan told his neighbours that he was happy and looking forward to the birth of his next child. In the evenings, he drank whisky with his friends and toasted the unborn child. It seems, however, that Alexander McCowan harboured a secret, and much darker, plan.

Since his return from the army, McCowan had also become secretly engaged to an attractive, fair-haired young lady named Catherine Robertson, whose family were well off enough to own a public house in Comrie. Among the social circles within Comrie, McCowan made no secret of his intention to marry Catherine, and that he expected to profit handsomely by the match. However, without first removing the obstacle of Alison and his child, he knew he could never marry Catherine. McCowan pleaded with Alison to leave him and take the child with her, but she refused, taunting him that she would never leave. Instead, McCowan knew he would be forced to provide for both her, his first child, and the (soon to be born) second child. Furious and seething with anger, McCowan hatched a plan to extract his terrible revenge on Alison, thus simultaneously freeing him to marry Catherine Robertson.

With his devious scheme in mind, he proposed marriage to Alison; telling her they would travel to Edinburgh, become man and wife, and start afresh there.

'Catherine Robertson is no longer the woman I desire', he told Alison, 'I have seen the light and now know deep down that you are the only woman I want.'

Delighted, and thinking that McCowan had experienced a change of heart, Alison excitedly told her friends of the proposal. She managed to borrow thirteen shillings (approximately £200 today) from friends and family to defray the expense of the marriage in Edinburgh.

Shortly afterwards, on a pleasant Saturday evening, sometime in early August 1749, as the sun was beginning to set, McCowan arrived back at their humble lodgings in Crieff (presumably after having secretly visited Catherine Robertson in Comrie). The couple waited until night fell, at which point they gathered their few paltry belongings and set out on the highway towards Edinburgh. Alison (despite being heavily pregnant) carried their youngest child on her back. When they reached the grounds of the Pitkellony Estate, well out of sight of any travellers on the road, McCowan advised Alison to climb over the dyke wall and rest, telling her she must be tired and weary with

the child on her back. It is likely that McCowan would have known the Pitkellony Estate well, as the laird, David Drummond, had hidden many Jacobite sympathisers there in the aftermath of the failed '45 uprising. Alexander McCowan undoubtedly also knew a quiet spot that could not be overseen. Once the couple had climbed within the enclosure, behind the cover of the dyke wall, McCowan pretended to show his concern and affection for Alison, pulling her near, and whispering softly to her. However, at that very moment, he drew his dirk (small dagger) and violently stabbed her in the back. Alison cried out in pain, but no one could hear her, and as she slumped forward, he stabbed her again. McCowan then cut the throat of his sleeping child with a razor. After rifling Alison's pocket for the remains of the thirteen shillings, he took the shift dress which she had been given for the marriage, together with a pair of her stockings. He then laid the two dead bodies together, covering them with her plaid, before finally camouflaging them with a layer of leaves, moss, and branches.

Under cover of darkness, he returned in great haste to Comrie and, rejoicing in the success of his plan, told the gruesome story in its entirety to Catherine Robertson. She also rejoiced, comforting McCowan by faithfully promising to never reveal his secret, and by reassuring him that he need not fear being discovered, as there had been no witnesses to the murders he had committed. Without witnesses, she assured him, he could not be convicted.

Thinking he had succeeded in his despicable crime, McCowan continued his relationship with Catherine for several weeks, until the arrival of Constable Murray and the angry posse of locals to arrest him, on the night of the dancing ball in late September.

Crucially, at his trial, the evidence of the shift dress and stockings that he had taken from his victim on the night of the murder, became important material evidence that eventually helped to convict him.

McCowan's execution was scheduled to be held at Perth on Monday 15th June, 1750. A large crowd had gathered, as was usual for a public execution. In a gruesome pre-hanging ritual, McCowan's right hand (the hand in which he had held the dirk to commit the murder) was placed on a block of wood and chopped off with an axe. A noose was then placed around his neck and the other end slung over the frame of the wooden gallows. At this time, hangings were not performed in such a way that the prisoner would be killed instantly. Instead of the more merciful 'drop hanging', with an elevated gallows and a drop hole for the convicted person to fall through, the prisoner was first placed on a cart pulled by a horse. After the noose had been placed around the prisoner's neck and secured to a branch above, the horse would be slapped and would slowly walk forward with the cart. Thus, instead of a quick, almost instantaneous, snap of the neck, the prisoner would be left to slowly strangle to death. It was not until nearly half a century later that the more 'humane' drop hole method of execution would become common practice in Scotland.

However, on this occasion, as the horse and cart were led away from under the hanging body, the rope snapped under his weight and McCowan fell to the ground still alive. Overjoyed, thinking he had escaped justice (this occurrence was often referred to as 'an act of God' or 'divine judgement' in which God had interjected to prevent a miscarriage of justice), McCowan fully expected to be released. However, his moment of relief soon passed, as another, stronger rope was quickly found. This time there was no reprieve, the rope held firm, and McCowan received his justice for the terrible and bloody murder of his partner, unborn baby, and child. His body was not immediately cut down, but left hanging and twisting in the breeze, until it was certain that he had expired.

In a bizarre footnote to the story, an interesting piece of urban folklore grew up around the macabre event. Once death had been proclaimed and McCowan's body taken down, the hangman cut up the noose into pieces and threw the lengths of rope into the crowd (it was considered good luck to catch and keep a piece of rope that had been used in a hanging). However, one of these lengths of cord hit a heavily pregnant woman standing in the crowd. It was reported, just a few days later, that she gave birth to a baby boy with its right hand missing.

THE BANTAM OF BOVAIN

In 1842 Queen Victoria and Prince Albert made their legendary visit to Taymouth Castle at Kenmore in Perthshire, to be entertained lavishly by Lord Breadalbane. To those lucky enough to be invited, it was an occasion to be talked about for years to come. However, to those who lived close by, another story dominated the early 1840s.

The bodies of three men, who all seemed to have suffered untimely deaths, were found in mysterious circumstances between the parishes of Kenmore and Killin; and all three were suitors of the same woman, Margaret Crerar. Margaret resided with her father at Bovain, near Killin; one of many branches of the Crerar family living on the north banks of Loch Tay at that time.

She was short and slight; and had become known locally as the 'Bantam of Bovain', after the name given to the smallest breed of chickens or fowl kept by the local farmers.

Neither was Margaret young; she was probably in her 40s. nor was she wealthy. However, she was considered highly desirable by many of the single men living on Lochtayside at that time. Margaret enjoyed their advances, even encouraged them, yet often expressed to her friends her desire to remain unmarried

John Campbell was a respected and wealthy local farmer. Aged 55, he was the owner of two farms in the region. Turai in Kenmore and Tullich, near Killin. John Campbell spent the majority of his time at Tullich, nestled on the slopes on the north side of Loch Tay, mainly due to his affection for Margaret Crerar and his wish to be near her. An elder of the local church, he was known as a sober and likeable man. He courted Margaret zealously, eventually asking her for her hand in marriage. Margaret's family seemed certain that she would accept, and even began planning a future wedding. Margaret, however, insisted on delaying her answer until she had returned from visiting relatives in the south.

Campbell, seemingly assuming the nuptials were a foregone conclusion, began planning enthusiastically. He purchased an expensive new wedding suit from a Perth tailor and brought in a supply of whisky and provisions from the county's finest merchants.

On the morning of Wednesday 15th January 1840 Campbell left his farm at Tullich, heading for Killin, to continue making arrangements for the impending wedding. He intended to visit Margaret at Bovain, then meet with the minister in Killin to organise the reading of the banns of marriage on the following sabbath. Campbell wore his new tartan plaid to protect himself from the cold, and to help conceal the large sum of money he was carrying (believed to be £80 – approximately £8,500 today).

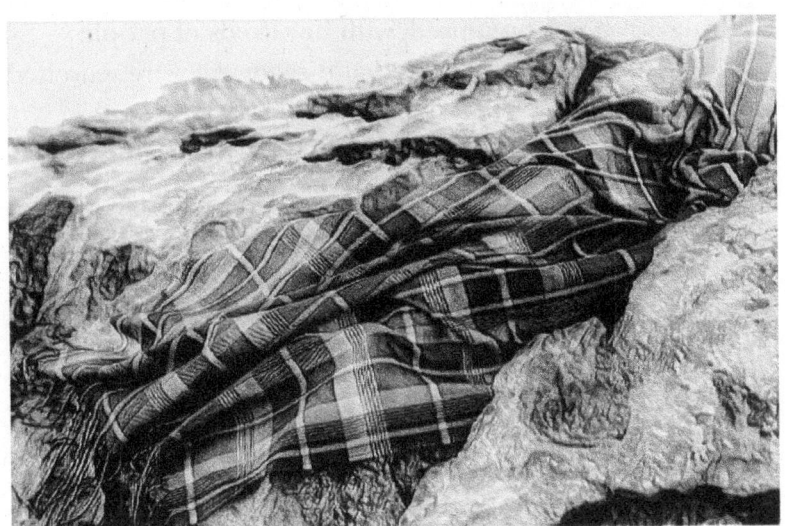

He was accompanied by two friends as far as Killin, where they enjoyed a whisky together at a local inn. The mood was jovial, and the men freely discussed the marriage arrangements. Next, Campbell visited his sister for afternoon tea and told her that he intended to call at the recently opened post office in Killin (perhaps to purchase the recently introduced penny black stamp and take advantage of the newly available postal service). He then intended to travel on to Bovain to set the exact date of the wedding ceremony.

Although he was seen by several witnesses heading in the general direction of Bovain, he never arrived there. Neither did he call into the local post office first. In fact, John Campbell was never seen alive again. When he did not return to his farm at Tullich, that evening, it was assumed that he had stayed the night at his sister's. However, when two further days had passed, his family began to worry.

A local search was organised, with hundreds of people agreeing to take part. The land and roadways were searched by a large group of able-bodied men. The waters of the river at Dochart, together with the banks surrounding Loch Tay, were also minutely examined, then dredged by boat. In accordance with Highland tradition, a party spent an overnight vigil on the hillsides overlooking the water. Local superstition told of a revealing light that would illuminate the spot at which a body was concealed beneath the water. However, their efforts were unsuccessful.

A detailed search was then carried out on the north side of Killin, for a stretch of more than two miles along the twisting road that sat beside the river from Dochart to Bovain. Despite searching for more than a week, their endeavours proved fruitless.

Finally, almost two weeks later, the diligence of the search parties was rewarded, when on Tuesday 28th January, at a spot between KIllin and Bovain, John Campbell's tartan plaid was spotted. The garment had become twisted and caught around a jagged rock, underneath the surface of the river, in an area close to the cottages at Craignavie. On examination, the cloth appeared to have several cuts in the material, which did not seem to have been made by the rocks. This finding reinvigorated the efforts of the search parties, organised by John Campbell's brother, who now felt certain that the body must have found its way into the water.

Another six weeks would pass until, almost two months after Campbell's disappearance, on Sunday 8th March 1840, his body was discovered lodged in a pool, near the beach, at the junction of the two rivers that flow into the west end of Loch Tay at Killin. The corpse had been bleached and disfigured from its long exposure to the water and was found face down on the riverbed. Campbell's body was removed from the water, and his clothing examined, whilst the authorities in Perth were sent for. His waistcoat was fully buttoned up, yet the shirt underneath was completely untucked. The pockets of his jacket were pulled inside out. This strange arrangement of his clothing did not seem to have been caused by the action of the moving water.

Campbell's pocketbook contained just £21 in notes, leaving approximately £59 unaccounted for. Following the search party's discovery, the body was strapped to a ladder and carefully replaced in the water, until the medical examiners from Perth arrived.

The two medical men from Perth, Dr Malcolm and Dr Thomson, minutely examined the body on the following day. Both doctors were able to declare that John Campbell's death had been caused by violence, stating 'murder was the cause'. The large wound to his skull appeared to have been caused by the shoe of a horse. In their report they also confirmed that 'the wounds were inflicted during life', and that Campbell was 'dead before he was put in the water'. An immediate investigation into his murder was then undertaken.

Local suspicion fell first on James McDougall, the keeper of the Toll-Bar at Lix, on the road leading from Lochearnhead to Killin. McDougall lived on the opposite bank of the Dochart River, in sight of Bovain, at a point where the river could be easily crossed. Although he was well liked and jovial in nature, McDougall was a large, and strong man, known locally to possess a violent temper. He was also rumoured to be involved in the local illicit whisky smuggling trade.

McDougall, it transpired, was also a suitor of Margaret Crerar. Indeed, he had already proposed marriage to her on several occasions. When McDougall had overheard talk of the intended marriage between Margaret Crerar and John Campbell, and when news first reached him of the proposed reading of their banns of marriage, he sent a note to Margaret stating that he urgently needed to speak to her. McDougall's note suggested they meet at an agreed spot just outside Bovain, on that Wednesday afternoon (the same day as John Campbell went missing). Margaret Crerar replied, agreeing to meet him, but suggested that James McDougall should bring some money with him, if his intentions towards her were serious.

On receiving her reply, McDougall rode as fast as his horse could carry him, from Lix Toll-Bar to Bovain, via Killin, despite later claiming that he had a sore leg which severely inhibited his ability to ride a horse. The journey of seven miles took him approximately 20 minutes and he arrived, his blood already boiling. He held tightly to his horse during the brief meeting. McDougall challenged Margaret Crerar, demanding to know if she intended to marry John Campbell. She replied that she did not. McDougall insisted that she had better not or else there would be consequences. However, Margaret refused to listen and turned to walk home. At this point McDougall remounted his horse and returned, riding furiously again, to Lix Toll-Bar.

The evening was rainy and stormy, although, at times, the moon shone brightly. On the road between Killin and Bovain, about a quarter of a mile from KIllin, stood two cottages known as Craignavie. The buildings were situated about 20 yards from the roadside and about 40 yards from the river. Around 10pm, on that windy and stormy night, the inhabitants of one of the cottages heard an eerie sound coming from the road. They described the sound as that of a person moaning. The strange noise stopped, then started again, lasting for about 15 minutes. The woman in the cottage described the moaning as 'like the sound of a friend crying in the distance', her husband 'as if it was the ghost of some person dying, the moaning was so unearthly.'

The man offered to go outside and find the source of the strange moaning, but his wife persuaded him not to. Had they done so, perhaps John Campbell may not have met his untimely death.

Two days later, when the search for the missing John Campbell began, James McDougall was asked to participate. He showed no interest in helping, however, claiming that his sore leg prevented him from doing so. McDougall also tried to dissuade the search parties from examining any of the banks bordering the river, claiming that they 'were wasting their time', and that Campbell's body 'could only be in the water'. McDougall also claimed that he suffered from 'falling fits of sickness', which would prevent him from assisting in the search. When told that John Campbell and Margaret Crerar were due to be married shortly, McDougall proclaimed 'that will not be!', and even offered a wager to anyone who disagreed with him.

Suspicion began to increase when John Campbell's body was recovered from the river. McDougall then admitted, when questioned, that he had been on the same road during the evening of Campbell's disappearance. He claimed, however, that he had seen no one except for a young lad he knew, who he noticed had a tartan plaid wrapped around his head. The young man was questioned but he denied being on the road at that time. He also stated that he was not in the habit of wearing a plaid around his head. John Campbell, the murdered man, on the other hand, was well known to wrap a plaid around his head to protect himself against the cold.

James McDougall was also seen by witnesses on the following day, wearing a greatcoat, which seemed to be cut and stained.

The disappearance and murder of John Campbell was investigated with much vigour by the authorities. The Procurator-Fiscal of Perthshire and the Sheriff Principal (Lord Anderson) were joined by the Deputy Advocate from Edinburgh, as a detailed investigation ensued. James McDougall was arrested on 6th March; however, the authorities did not conclude their enquiries until 10th August, more than five months later. McDougall remained incarcerated throughout this time.

During the entire period of his imprisonment McDougall

insisted that another man, who was in service at Bovain, was to blame. The young man apparently was also in love with Margaret Crerar. Unfortunately for James McDougall, the young man could not be traced as he too had mysteriously gone missing on the very same night.

The thorough investigation by the Procurator-Fiscal's office concluded that James McDougall may well have returned to Bovain on the evening of 15th January and, seeing John Campbell on the road, rode him down with his powerful horse. Campbell's body was then dragged into the undergrowth, at the roadside, and left for dead (this may have accounted for traces of earth found on the tartan plaid). It was assumed that McDougall had then traversed the river later that night, at a shallow crossing point near his home on the opposite side of the bank; and disposed of the body in the river. Possibly taking some of the money from the pockets of the dead man's coat. This may well have explained the moaning heard by the occupants of the cottages at Craignavie during that night.

However, the theory was problematic and lacked any substantiating evidence. McDougall had not been seen on the road by anyone that evening. None of the missing money was found at his home, or about his person. Nor had he been seen spending an unusually large amount of money in any of the shops or inns nearby. In addition, witnesses were able to testify that he had definitely been at home at 7pm that evening (although, of course, he could have gone out later).

Despite the long investigation McDougall was eventually

released without trial and without charge. The murder of John Campbell remained unsolved.

Margaret Crerar continued to receive suitors and offers of marriage after the tragic events of 1840. Life returned to normal in Killin, until three years later – almost to the day – two further mysterious deaths devastated the small town. Both men were found face down in the water and both were rumoured to have been suitors of Miss Crerar.

During the evening of Friday 27th January 1843, John McIntosh, a game-herd working in Glendochart, attended a wedding at the remote and isolated Lix-Toll House, near Killin. He had danced with Margaret Crerar during the celebrations, then left to travel home on foot in the dark later that evening. John McIntosh was never seen alive again. His body was not discovered until 7th February, face down in almost the same spot at the west end of Loch Tay, that John Campbell's body had been found in three years earlier. A similar investigation ensued, and the following conclusion was reached by the authorities:

And, whereas, from the appearances on the body, and many other circumstances, there is reason to believe that the said John McIntosh was, at an hour early on the morning of the 28th January last, MURDERED.

Just a few weeks later, on 19th February, the body of yet another man was found, drowned and face down, in a small pool near Drummond Castle, just outside Crieff. The man was identified, 'as a dyer by trade and having come from Killin'. It was thought that the man had recently travelled to Crieff, from Killin, to visit family and to inform them of his impending marriage to Margaret Crerar. He had been known locally to have courted Margaret Crerar for several weeks. With no evidence of foul play, however, the matter could not be taken any further.

Meanwhile, the authorities, still investigating the previous murder of John McIntosh, were unable to find a culprit, so placed a notice in the Perthshire newspapers asking for assistance:

A REWARD OF ONE HUNDRED POUNDS
Is hereby offered to be paid by
HER MAJESTY'S GOVERNMENT,
to any person who shall, within one month
from this date, give such information as shall lead
to the discovery and conviction of the Person or Persons
concerned in the Murder of the said
John Mcintosh.
And FURTHER, Her Majesty has been advised to grant
A GRACIOUS PARDON
To any Accomplice, not being the Person
who actually committed the Murder,
who shall give such information,
as shall lead to the same result.

By instruction from Her Majesty's Principal Secretary
Of State For The Home Department,
ROBERT WHIGHAM,
Sheriff of Perthshire, Perth, 19th April, 1843.

Sadly, despite the substantial reward of £100 offered (today's equivalent of more than £12,000), it appears that the murders were never solved, and the story remains wrapped in mystery.

The land on the north side of Loch Tay, between Killin and Kenmore, which once boosted a bustling population of more than 3,500 people, including a large number of Crerars, saw its numbers hugely eroded, over the next 50 years, due to economic migration and the Highland Clearances. Many members of that family eventually emigrated to Nova Scotia.

James McDougall was always regarded suspiciously, despite no crime being proved against him. Not long after the two suspicious deaths in 1843, he married another local girl.

However, soon after the wedding, he too died suddenly. Still a young man at the time, and seemingly in good health, no cause of death could be determined, and the matter remained a mystery.

Margaret Crerar remained unmarried and lived into old age, dying peacefully many years later.

THE DYING MURDERER

During the early hours of Sunday 26th October 1930, the calm of a chilly autumn night was broken at the Newton of Huntingtower farm, just outside Perth. The farm was situated adjacent to the road between Perth and Crieff; and a sizeable distance across the fields to the new corporation housing development at Tulloch. A sizeable enough distance to prevent anyone from hearing a scream. The farm was dark, with only the distant twinkling of lights coming from the city of Perth, a mile or so across the fields. The new electricity grid, which had begun to illuminate the towns and cities of Scotland, had not yet reached the farm.

Around 4am in the morning Cathy Peddie, a young dairymaid at the farm, was awoken by the sound of the sheepdogs barking. It was not particularly unusual for the dogs to bark and ordinarily Cathy would have thought little of it, other than her usual annoyance at being woken. However, in the quiet of the night she distinctly heard two voices, that seemed to emanate from the farmyard. The residents of the farm were used to being disturbed by the sound of vagrants, who often slept in the outbuildings, or passed by in the dead of the night. After a few moments the voices stopped and, hearing nothing further, she fell back into a slumber.

An hour later, around 5am, Mr John Guthrie who, together with his father, managed the farm left the main farmhouse and headed across the yard to the byre, to prepare for morning milking. It was a chilly and misty morning, and still cold. The sun had not risen; and the farmyard was cloaked in darkness. He overheard a woman's voice coming from the cart shed. Guthrie assumed the sound was likely to be a vagrant. There had been many using the farm's sheds for shelter in the recent weeks. John Guthrie resolved to turn them out after he had finished milking and the sun had come up.

He returned to the cart shed around 7am, the sun was just beginning to illuminate the sky away to the east, but it was not yet fully light. As his eyes gradually became accustomed to the half-light a horrific sight greeted him. It was evident that two people had slept on the large pile of straw, in one corner of the shed. However, a vivid red trail of blood led from the straw, across the shed, to the opposite wall. As he turned his head, his eyes following the trail, he saw the body of what appeared to be a woman slumped in the far corner. Her body was stretched out across the floor, with just her head propped up against the wall. Her body, from the shoulders downwards, had been concealed with an overcoat but her face and neck remained uncovered. There was a large gash across the throat and her face had been horrifically mutilated. Blood from the wounds had evidently gushed from her throat, saturating the straw on the ground. The victim's hands were also heavily stained with blood. Despite the dim light and her badly disfigured face, a look of terror remained on the poor woman's face. John Guthrie jumped back in horror and ran from the shed into the light, his heart pounding.

Recovering his composure, he telephoned Police Constable McIntosh, from Almondbank, who was first on the scene. PC McIntosh, in turn, called Inspector Davidson, from Perth City Police Headquarters, and Mr Matthew Martin, the Chief Constable. The terrible nature of the crime shocked all those present; and suicide was immediately ruled out as a cause of death. No one present thought it likely that a person would have been able to inflict wounds of that nature upon themselves. The injuries to the body appeared to have been caused by an extremely sharp instrument, perhaps a cutthroat razor or small pocketknife. An immediate search of the crime scene was undertaken and a search for the perpetrator initiated. The officers were unable to locate anything that resembled a likely murder weapon in the immediate vicinity. However, several large, bloodstained stones were discovered on the floor of the cart shed. The perpetrator had not left any other tangible clues at the scene. There were no recognisable footprints nor discarded items that might lead to an obvious suspect. Neither did the victim have any identification on her person that might offer the police officers a vital clue.

Searches were made of all the outlying farm buildings, as well as the surrounding fields. When this proved fruitless, the search was extended to neighbouring farms. Roadblocks were set up and motor cars travelling to and from Crieff were stopped and searched. Statements were taken from the residents of the few scattered homes and farms in the vicinity. None of these householders could recall seeing, or hearing, anything unusual, either early that morning or during the previous day.

By mid-afternoon, word of the brutal murder had reached Perth. There had been no reports of a missing woman filed at any of the police stations in the area; although given that the location of the murder was commonly used by vagrants and travellers, police did not think that unusual.

Meanwhile, the officers involved in the case had re-convened in the detectives' office at Perth police station, ready to discuss their next move. The discussion was animated. Should they involve the press in their hunt for the killer? Should they widen the breadth of the search? Were they hunting for one person in particular; and who was the victim? Her mutilated body would need to be thoroughly cleaned before a formal identification could take place.

At that very moment a poorly-dressed and extremely dirty vagrant, with a large unkempt moustache and long untidy hair, walked into the police station – just a few yards from where the detectives were meeting. He was wearing bloodstained clothing, carrying two small bags, and seemed to be wandering aimlessly in a state of disorientation and distress. It did not take the officers long to make the connection between the man and the body of the dead woman at the Newton of Huntingtower farm.

Alexander Isdale Mitchell had been a recognisable character on the streets of Perth for many years. A well-known vagrant and street 'pedlar' (an archaic occupation which required a licence from the authorities), Mitchell had often been seen wandering the streets of the Fair City selling whatever items he could lay his hands on, from pegs and clothes, to matches or cigarettes. He was commonly seen sleeping rough with his wife Christina Mitchell, in sheltered alleyways or outbuildings around the city and the surrounding locales. Alexander Mitchell was 5'5", with pale, dirty skin, and a rasping cough. He looked considerably older than his 49 years.

When asked about the murder at the Newton of Huntingtower farm, Mitchell did not openly admit the offence; but became noticeably furtive and agitated. He could not explain how he his clothing had become bloodstained; and he remained tight-lipped over the location of his wife Christine. His general behaviour was erratic and his answers to the officers' questions incoherent. With no other suspects or known motive for the murder, the police saw an opportunity for a speedy resolution to the case.

In today's climate, Alexander Mitchell might well have been offered immediate psychiatric counselling and, at a very minimum, legal support. However, the case seemed an open-and-shut one and Mitchell's strange behaviour and seemingly carefree attitude convinced the detectives of his guilt.

At that time, a suspect did not necessarily have the right to be represented by legal counsel at the time of arrest. This privilege was often only afforded to those able to finance that burden themselves. Gradually, during the second half of the 20th century this right was extended to cover the period from arrest to trail, up to and including the court of appeal.

In the case of Alexander Mitchell, however, he was arrested and formally charged as follows:

That on Saturday 25th or Sunday 26th October 1930, in the cart shed at the Steading at Newton of Huntingtower Farm, near Perth, occupied by Mr Charles Guthrie, farmer, did assault your wife Christina McFayden, or Mitchell, and cut her on the face, hands, throat and body, with a razor or other sharp instrument, and did murder her.

Officers checked to make sure that Mitchell understood the severity of the charges, at which point he was transferred to Perth Prison to be kept on remand while a date was set for his trial. Meanwhile the investigation and case were prepared for the High Court.

The officers involved had a very good reason for proceeding in such haste with the case against Alexander Mitchell. Unfortunately, Mitchell's health was poor. So poor, in fact, it was thought he may not survive long enough to face justice.

Meanwhile, the damp and uncomfortable cell at Perth Prison exacerbated Mitchell's symptoms. He had recently undergone an operation for bowel cancer, which had not been successful. Coupled with liver damage caused by his excessive drinking, and the harsh conditions he was forced to endure on a daily basis, doctors predicted that he may only have a matter of weeks left to live. He was transferred to the slightly more comfortable surroundings of Murthly District Asylum in the hope of an improvement.

Despite the brutal nature of the murder, there were some public reservations about Mitchell's mental and physical state, and his readiness to face trial. However, notwithstanding those concerns, a High Court date for Mitchell's trial was set for Tuesday 2nd February 1931. Mitchell, it seemed, would have to spend three months on remand.

As the weeks passed by, Mitchell also appeared to suffer from a rapid decline in his capacity to understand the investigation into his wife's murder, or the seriousness of the charges facing him. There was also a noticeable decline in his cognitive powers and his mental health generally. Following a petition from doctors at the Asylum, and the evidence of medical witnesses, Mitchell entered a plea of 'insanity, at the time of the murder'. Fortunately, an early form of legal aid had recently been introduced in Scotland, enabling Mitchell to receive at least some helpful advice and the basis of a sound defence at his trial.

At Mitchell's hearing in Perth, several witnesses and experts testified that he had no recollection whatsoever of the tragic events at the farm. He could not remember arriving at the farm with his wife, the murder itself, wandering from the farm after the killing, walking into Perth City Police

Station, or being arrested by the police. An examination by Dr Chambers, Mitchell's doctor at Murthly District Asylum, was read out to the court in evidence, in which it was declared that Mitchell would be unable to understand any of the charges being read to him, nor make sense of the proceedings.

Faced with overwhelming medical evidence, the lack of any other suspect, Mitchell's rapidly deteriorating health, and his state of mind, Lord Murray accepted the plea of insanity and ordered that Mitchell be detained at His Majesty's pleasure indefinitely.

He was taken from the court, where several hundred people had gathered outside to witness for themselves the brutal murderer of Christina Mitchell before his transfer to Perth Prison.

Mitchell's health did, indeed, fail. During the next few weeks, he was transferred back and forth between Perth Royal Infirmary and the prison before eventually passing away on Monday 21st September 1931. Mitchell was never able to fully comprehend the events surrounding his wife's death, nor the seriousness of his crime. In fact, it was reported that he frequently asked the prison warders why Christine had not visited him.

Alexander Mitchell's life had been a hard one. Born in Old Machar in Aberdeen, one of seven siblings, money had always been short. His father and brother had both suffered from mental illness and were ultimately admitted to Aberdeen Royal Asylum; Mitchell's father eventually committing suicide. Following the end of the Great War, his brother also took his own life; never fully able to come to terms with his experiences on the Western Front. Mitchell's own history had also been a difficult one, with little in the way of employment opportunities, exacerbated by his history of poor health, a disturbed home life, vagrancy, and alcoholism.

He had married Christina in 1920. The couple had wandered the countryside, often sleeping rough, scratching a living wherever they could. As the recession had started to bite in 1930, Mitchell had found it increasingly hard to obtain work of any kind, eventually resorting to even more bouts of heavy drinking as his only escape.

The examination by Dr Chambers (undertaken for the court) had declared that:

He was a man of limited intelligence and his conduct had shown defective judgement and defective moral control. Mitchell's intellectual age did not exceed nine years.

So why did Mitchell suddenly snap and so brutally kill his wife of 10 years? It appears that she, too, drank to excess, often becoming unruly and difficult. Christina had been fined on several occasions by Perth Sheriff Court, usually on public order charges. The fines had caused Alexander Mitchell a great deal of trouble. He had been forced to work, in order to pay the fines, leaving the couple with little food and no money for accommodation. On the day before the murder, the couple had been asked to leave the Poorhouse Hospital but had argued over where they might best go in the hope of finding somewhere warm to spend the night. Christina had wanted to go to Bankfoot, Mitchell to Almondbank. After several disagreements they had finally ended up deciding to spend the night in the cart shed at the Newton of Huntingtower farm.

What happened then to cause this sudden and violent attack will never be fully known. Did Mitchell deliberately kill his wife, as an intentional act of revenge for the miserable life for which he blamed her; realising that he did not have long to live? Was the killing of Christina Mitchell premeditated, or a moment's flash of uncontrollable anger? Did he manage to dupe the authorities, feign his insanity and, knowing all along that his terminal illness would probably help him avoid the death penalty, no matter what the outcome of his trial? That seems unlikely, however, knowing his prolonged history of hospital admissions and the ample witness testimony. Yet, he did have the foresight to cover the body with an overcoat and discard the murder weapon (which was never found), then quickly leave the scene of the crime.

It seems most likely that Mitchell snapped in a moment of intense psychosis, caused by a lifetime of alcohol abuse, hardship and misery. Whatever the reason, it is the truly heart-breaking story of two sad and wasted lives.

Alexander Mitchell was interred in Perth's Wellshill Cemetery and his wife's body returned to her family in Buckhaven, in Fife, where she was buried.

THE KILLING OF JANET SMITH
(PART ONE)

2024 marks the 100th anniversary of the killing of a young girl from Perth that sent shockwaves around the world. The death of Janet Smith was so notorious, so scandalous, and so controversial, that it stunned the people of Canada for many years. Her death rocked polite society, led to long standing political and legal ramifications, and remains the most intriguing and enigmatic unsolved murder in Canadian history.

Yet the story of the nursemaid from Perth in Scotland, who travelled 6,000 miles to meet her grizzly end, is hardly known in her hometown. Despite money being raised in Perth, to contribute towards both her memorial in Vancouver and the subsequent investigation into her death (undertaken largely by Scottish police officers), Janet Smith's name has now been largely forgotten in

Scotland.

Interest in the story was once so acute in Perth that news of the drama played out daily in the Perth and Dundee newspapers, thanks to regular telegrams despatched from Vancouver. Attitudes prevalent in the 1920s helped shape public opinion on the case in both Scotland and Canada and almost led to a shocking miscarriage of justice. The drama also reveals uncomfortable truths about racist attitudes prevailing at the time (in both Scotland and Canada) and forced Canadian society to re-examine, and re-think, its own part in the sad affair. Whilst the events were well documented in Canada, we are now able to add to the story, for the first time, details only reported in Perth and the part played in influencing public opinion by the Scottish Societies in Vancouver. Here, then, is the tale of Canada's most infamous unsolved murder.

Janet Kennedy Smith was born on 25th June 1902 at 105 Scott Street in Perth, to a family of modest means. Her father, Arthur Mitchell Smith, was employed as a railway fireman at Perth General railway station, then later at Garvie and Deas in South Methven Street. Her mother, Johanna, was Norwegian. Despite her mixed heritage the press would later dub her 'The Scottish Nightingale'. The youngest of six children, Janet grew up in a busy but happy household, where neighbours described her as 'an exceptionally nice girl, bright and happy, with a sweet disposition. She impressed everyone with her gentleness and kindness.'

After finishing school Janet obtained a certificate to

be a nursemaid (what would now be called a nanny). At the age of 19 she began to seek employment in that profession, hoping to find a wealthy couple with whom she could enjoy security and perhaps travel. Firstly, she found employment as a nursemaid to Rev McNaughton in Barnhill, Perth, alongside her sister Mary-Ann, who was already employed there as a cook. Then, in January 1923, Doreen and Frederick Lefevre Baker, a wealthy Scottish/Canadian couple who lived in Kensington, advertised and hired Janet to care for their new-born baby. When Lefevre-Baker's importing business took the family to Paris, Janet moved with them. Baker was a wealthy man, a former flyer in the Royal Air Force and son-in-law of another Scottish Canadian, General Alexander Macrae, a millionaire lumberman from Ottawa. In October 1923 the Bakers returned to Vancouver and managed to entice Janet to move with them, by the generous offer of a monthly salary of not less than $30 (approximately £850 today) and the guarantee of a return ticket to Scotland, should she not find the country to her liking.

They moved into a house in the city's fashionable West End, a location that gave Janet access to nearby Stanley Park, where she often took the baby for strolls. Here she found it easy to meet members of Vancouver's bachelor community. She was taken to the cinema and received gifts of chocolates from admirers. Janet soon developed relationships that ranged from flirtatious to serious.

Janet (known to her friends as Nettie) kept a detailed diary in which she revealed her musings on her own sexuality and romantic desires. Many of the entries were decidedly melodramatic - 'Heavenly night, immense moon and nobody nice to love me' - others are cryptic - 'I suppose I will always play with fire. I expect that is what the fortune teller meant when she said I have the girdle of Venus.' Since Janet fully intended to return to Britain, she often reproached herself for leading men along, yet also seemed to be concerned with the idea of remaining a respectable girl. Her diary entries reveal her to be a far more complex figure than the one the Vancouver press would later construct.

In May 1924 Janet moved with the Bakers into the home of Baker's brother, Richard, at 3851 Osler Avenue, in the elite Shaughnessy Heights neighbourhood of Point Grey (then a separate municipality, south of Vancouver). There she worked alongside the Baker's 'houseboy' and servant, Wong Foon Sing. 25-year-old Wong was an immigrant from Hong Kong and a diligent worker who laboured hard in order to send money home to his wife in China. The relationship between Janet Smith and Wong would become the subject of much discussion after her death. Although her friends testified that she feared he would murder her, her diary reveals that Wong gave her intimate presents such as a silk nightdress, was smitten with her, and that she was well aware of the effect she had on him. Her diary clearly disclosed the enjoyment she felt from her undoubted appeal to the other sex.

On the morning of 26th July 1924, Wong was peeling potatoes in the kitchen when he heard what he thought was a car backfiring. He looked out of the kitchen window into the street but could see nothing, so he decided to go down to the basement to investigate. Here he found Janet Smith lying lifeless on the cement floor next to the ironing board, her head partly underneath the laundry tub, which stood on a plinth. She was clothed in her pale blue denim uniform. A rivulet of blood was streaming from a bullet wound in her right temple, matting her thick, blonde hair. Under her arm was the cord from the electric iron, which it appeared had been pulled from the socket above the ironing board as she fell; and come to rest against the right side of her body. A .45 automatic pistol lay near her outstretched hand, as did her smashed reading glasses.

According to Wong Foon Sing's testimony he was the only person in the house (apart from the Baker's infant son) when the shooting allegedly occurred. Wong telephoned Frederick Baker – who was at work - to report the grisly discovery. At 12.30pm Baker, in turn, contacted the police. Point Grey Police Constable James Green was immediately despatched to the house. However, at the time of Mr Baker's telephone call to the police at Point Grey Police Station, he would not have been aware that the inexperienced Constable Green was the only officer available to answer the call. The Vancouver area was suffering a heatwave and many of the more senior officers had removed themselves to Bowen Island for their annual picnic. Meanwhile Chief Constable Hiram Simpson was catnapping in the cool back office. Constable Green was an overweight, 50-year-old officer, who had been stripped of the higher rank of Chief Detective seven years earlier, during a department reorganisation. Unable to find any other employment, he re-enlisted as a constable. Within four years of Janet Smith's killing, he would be employed as a night watchman at a local hospital.

On his arrival at Osler Ave (just 15 minutes after Frederick Baker's phone call to the station) Constable Green was met by Mr Baker and Wong Foon Sing, who was now wearing a heavy alpaca coat, fully buttoned up, despite the sultry conditions. The police constable was shown around the side of the house and down to the laundry room. He examined the body (moving it in the process) and noticed burns on her arm and a stain on her finger. Wong told the doctor that he had knelt over her body, listening for a heartbeat. On realising there was none, he had telephoned Mr Baker, his employer.

Crucially, Police Constable Green picked up the weapon, making it impossible to obtain any fingerprints from it. Despite there being no blood or brain tissue on the walls, no powder burns on her face, and the fact that the back of her head appeared to have suffered some form of blunt force trauma, Constable Green concluded that she had committed suicide.

Whilst it appeared that Janet was in the middle of ironing the infant's clothes, it was conjectured that she had chosen to stop abruptly and, either, suddenly decided to commit suicide, or to examine the pistol and accidently shot herself. Any hypothesis made at that time seemingly assumed that the pistol was stored in the basement. However, this assumption transpired to be erroneous, as it was later revealed that the gun was hidden in a haversack in the attic.

Had Janet chosen to suddenly commit suicide, this would have meant her going upstairs, entering the attic, locating the gun (if she was even aware of its existence), before returning to the basement with the gun and then shooting herself. Constable Green also failed to locate the bullet, which may have helped establish the angle of trajectory. This was not discovered until later. Dr Blackwood was called, who confirmed Janet Smith was dead, estimating the time of death to be within the previous four or five hours. He noted that the body was still warm (as was the iron). However, the extremely hot weather, and the stifling temperatures inside the cramped laundry room, may well have preserved her core body heat for longer than was usual. By the time a senior officer arrived the crime scene had been significantly disturbed, making a forensic examination problematic.

Despite these anomalies, at the hurried inquest the Vancouver coroner reported a 'self-inflicted but accidental death' after (as the newspapers were anxious to point out) 'the Chinaman was given the severest of examinations.' The verdict of accidental death also prevented two fundamental, but crucial, questions from being asked. Firstly, was Janet Smith aware of the presence of the pistol in the house? And secondly, did Wong Foon Sing know Janet was in the basement before hearing the sound of the shot? Or had he merely gone to the basement to investigate the noise?

Undertakers were then summoned, and instructed by both the Point Grey Coroner and the police to embalm the body, therefore eradicating any clues that a post mortem might have yielded, for instance whether Janet Smith had been sexually assaulted. It would later transpire that the undertaker had never before been asked to embalm the victim of a violent death without a post mortem being first carried out. In fact, the undertaker found unexplained burns on Janet Smith's right side, which he assumed where caused by the hot iron landing by her side, but his findings were not reported; as the cause of death was not deemed to be suspicious. After the embalming process, the body of Janet Smith was sent back to the morgue, where Dr Hunter decided to examine her embalmed corpse. He noted that there was no gunshot residue or burn marks around the entry hole, meaning the gun must have been fired from a distance, making suicide or an accident seemingly impossible.

Constable Green, who had moved the body thereby destroying vital evidence, was suspended, but later reinstated. He also later changed his opinion on the cause of death from suicide to accidental death, following the inquest.

Janet Smith was buried at Mountain View Cemetery in Vancouver and the sad saga seemed to be at an end. Interestingly, Janet's fellow nursemaids did not attend her funeral. They felt uneasy around the Baker family, who they believed were somehow responsible for her death. The Bakers, on the other hand, seemed to accept the verdict of accidental death without question and Wong Foon Sing continued in their employ.

The conclusion reached by the inquest, however, was just the beginning.

Several of Janet's friends, including fellow nursemaids Cissie Jones, Jean Haddowe and Mary Jones, refused to believe the verdict of suicide. Indeed, Jean Haddowe was approached by the Point Grey Police and asked to identify the body. She told the police officers present that Janet Smith could not have taken her own life, despite the officers insisting that she had taken her own life. The nursemaids had often met up with Janet Smith at Angus Park and they would regularly push their prams together to Cunningham's Drug Store on Granville Street for refreshments. Just the previous day, Janet Smith had paid a professional photographer to take a series of portraits of her. Hardly the act of someone about to take their own life. Scottish newspapers also reported that Janet was saving up enough money to travel back to Britain and visit her mother. Neither Cissie nor Jean believed that Janet Smith would ever kill herself. Janet was a popular and happy girl and had recently joined the Scots' Girls of Vancouver Society. Both Cissie and Jean stated that she had been uncomfortable around Wong Foon Sing, who – they claimed - was smitten by the nursemaid, calling her by the pet name 'Nursie'. Mary Jones also informed the authorities that during the course of her conversations with Janet Smith, the dead nursemaid had told her on several occasions that she was 'annoyed with the Chinese boy' and that she was 'so afraid of him.'

They enlisted the aid of two powerful organisations, the Vancouver United Council of Scottish Societies, and the Presbyterian Church, in the form of leader Reverend Duncan McDougall (who was concerned with the alleged moral perils caused by Chinese immigrants, particularly when directed towards young girls). The Scottish Societies sent telegrams to provincial Attorney General Alexander Malcolm Manson demanding that the case be reopened. Ultimately, however, it was *Vancouver Star* publisher Victor Wentworth Odlum who provided the impetus to have the case reopened. The *Vancouver Star* published a series of scandalous stories about the 'puzzling death' and apparent bungling by the police which stirred up intense interest; and pointed to Wong Foon Sing as the likely culprit.

Odlum was an 'exclusionist' who believed that Asians could not assimilate with whites. He had previously stood on an anti-Asian platform in the 1921 federal election. On 8th August, he published an editorial headed *Should Chinese Work with White Girls?* Odlum also publicly called for legislation to 'preserve white girls of impressionable youth from the unnecessary wiles and villainies of low-caste yellow men.'

Other Vancouver papers followed Odlum's lead and made Janet Smith's death a cause célèbre. Regular communication from the Canadian Scottish Societies ensured the story received lurid coverage in the Perth and Dundee newspapers. The Vancouver *Daily Star* carried the sensational headline *Nurse's Death Puzzle – Suicide Death Theory Is Not Satisfactory!*

Mounting public pressure led to the exhumation of her body on 28th August and a second inquest in September. This time a post-mortem, carried out by six doctors, revealed causes for concern. These included details of severe trauma to the victim's head, which were not caused by the bullet wound. A closer examination of Janet's head revealed that her scalp had been separated from her skull, and her cranium cracked. (The head injury had been originally explained away by assuming that, after she had pulled the trigger, Janet had fallen and hit her head on the laundry tub). It was impossible to ascertain whether the gunshot or head injury had occurred first, partly because of the embalming process and partly due to the passage of time since the incident.

It was also recorded that, in the opinion of the pathologist, the body appeared to have been re-dressed after death. The soles of her feet were matted with blood, yet no corresponding stains were present on the insides of her white canvas shoes. In addition, the burns on the right side of her body (previously presumed to have been caused by the hot iron falling from the ironing board) were not matched by any corresponding scorch marks on her clothing. Had the burn marks on her torso been caused in some other way and the story of the hot iron been manufactured afterwards to explain them away? Could an electric iron really be hot enough to burn the skin, through layers of clothing, without leaving the slightest scorch mark on the victim's outfit? It is notoriously difficult to dress a corpse and the process usually leaves tell-tale signs.

The separation of her scalp from her skull also seemed to be a highly unusual injury. None of the doctors present at the post-mortem had ever seen such an injury caused by a fall, only by trauma from a blow by a heavy instrument. The absence of powder burns around the gunshot wound also seemed to indicate the bullet may have been fired from a distance of several feet, rather than at close range.

The public in both Vancouver and in Perth waited on tenterhooks for the inquest's verdict.

THE KILLING OF JANET SMITH
(PART TWO)

The four-day inquest in the killing of Janet Smith recorded the following verdict:

We find that Janet K Smith was on, July 26th 1924, wilfully murdered in the course of her employment in the laundry basement at 3851 Osler Avenue, Vancouver, BC by being shot through the head by a revolver, but by whom fired we have no evidence to show. It is regrettable that the reading of picked extracts from the deceased's diary tended to defame her pure and unsullied memory.

The Scottish Societies in Vancouver vowed to keep up the pressure on the authorities to find the killer and wrote to the *Perthshire Advertiser* and *Dundee Courier* urging them to help keep the case in the public eye. Every effort was made to represent Janet Smith as a pure and innocent girl, while rumour, hearsay and innuendo were used to cast suspicion on Wong Foon Sing. Many questions were asked in the Scottish press: Why hadn't her fellow nursemaids been believed? Why weren't Janet's diaries examined properly by the police? (If they had been, it would have been noticed that Janet had purchased a new brooch on the day before her death; and arranged to telephone a young suitor –

neither seeming to be the act of someone about to take their own life). The case attracted worldwide interest, and the Chinese Council in Vancouver reported the matter to the Chinese Government in Peking (now Beijing).

A murder investigation was launched and Scottish police Inspector Forbes Cruickshank -formerly of the Aberdeen Police and now head of the Vancouver division of the BC Provincial Police - was placed in charge. Cruickshank could find no evidence or motive of suicide, immediately making Wong Foon Sing his prime suspect. He, in turn, contracted private detective Oscar Robinson, instructing him to follow Wong and obtain whatever information he could.

Oscar Robinson tailed Wong to learn his routines and habits, including who he visited in Vancouver's Chinatown (Wong was apparently aware that he was being followed, but did not seem to be particularly concerned). On the evening of Tuesday 12th August 1924, Wong stepped off the street-car at the corner of Cordova and Carrall Street, where he had planned to meet two friends. As they were talking, a large black automobile pulled up alongside, two burly white men leapt out, and forced Wong into the back of their car.

Wong Foon Sing was sure that he had been grabbed by vigilantes; intent on killing him in retribution for the death of Janet Smith. He was relieved when, instead, he was told he was being taken to the detective bureau. However, this turned out to be Oscar Robinson's Canadian Detective Bureau, contained in a cheaply furnished two room suite on West Hastings Street, where Oscar Robinson and his associates subjected Wong to an intense interrogation (which they called 'close questioning'). Wong explained that he had already told the police and the inquest everything he knew. Robinson beat him through the night, but Wong's story did not change. The men eventually forced Wong to sign a piece of paper, which he was unable to read as he could not understand written English. He suspected, however, that he had been forced to sign a false confession.

Seemingly satisfied, Wong was released by Oscar Robinson.

An appeal was launched by the Scottish Societies, across the Atlantic Ocean in Perth, to help raise funds to enable investigators to determine what had happened to 'the girl from the Old Country.' Scottish newspapers advised any parents of girls planning to work in Canada not to place them in households where Chinese servants were employed. The Scottish Societies also lobbied Vancouver politician Mary Ellen Smith to introduce legislation to prohibit employers from hiring both white women and 'Orientals' as servants in the same household. In November 1924 Mary Ellen Smith introduced the so-called 'Janet Smith Bill' (in fact, an amendment to the existing Women's and Girls' Protection Act of 1923). However, the bill failed to become law, following concerns over its legality at the British Columbia Legislature.

Despite efforts from the Scottish Societies, the case largely disappeared from the newspapers, until a shocking event occurred in Shaughnessy Heights. Wong Foon Sing suddenly vanished in March 1925; and newspapers in

Canada and in Scotland immediately leapt on this as proof of his guilt. Instead of reporting the fact that he had merely disappeared, Scottish Newspapers carried the headline:

> *PERTH GIRL'S TRAGIC DEATH:*
> *CHINESE SERVANT DISAPPEARS*
> *A Chinese servant at the Vancouver house*
> *where Janet Smith was murdered has disappeared.*
> *It is believed he has been smuggled away to China.*

The truth, however, was even more shocking. On 20th March 1925 a group of men dressed in Ku Klux Klan robes arrived at the Baker residence and abducted Wong Foon Sing (these men were later identified as operatives hired by the Scottish Societies, together with some off-duty police constables). The gang tied, gagged and blindfolded Wong, then drove him to a house on West 25th Avenue where, for six weeks, he was chained to the floor and tortured in an attempt to force him to confess, or to provide enough information, to explain Janet Smith's death. Eventually after six weeks, with Wong still refusing to change his story, he was dumped blindfolded, dazed, battered, and disoriented, on Marine Drive. It was now 1st May. It had been rumoured that the police knew of Wong's incarceration but did nothing, hoping that he would confess.

Unbelievably, Point Grey Police then promptly arrested Wong for the murder of Janet Smith. It appears they may have been 'tipped off' to Wong's location by the kidnappers and driven straight to Marine Drive to detain him. His arrest was reported in Scotland – 'Chinaman Sent For Trial'. No correction was made for the earlier false assumption that he had been smuggled back to China; instead, it was merely noted that 'Wong said he been kidnapped and that efforts had been made to extort information from him. Police investigations ended in his arrest.'

Despite his obvious injuries from his forced incarceration and torture, Wong was interrogated at length by the police and charged with the murder of Janet Smith. Newspapers in Perthshire reported Wong's 'strange story of being kidnapped by five men' with only a cursory mention of the physical injuries he suffered, which did seem to add credence to his story.

On the morning of 7th May 1925, the Municipal Hall in Kerrisdale was thronging with excited onlookers. The trial of Wong Foon Sing had attracted enormous public interest, with the courthouse packed. Women in the gallery even brought packed lunches with them, so as not to lose their seat in court during the lunch hour. Those who could not gain entry stared through the windows, their faces pressed against the window-panes. Wong was defended at trial by John Harold Senkler, a prominent lawyer who had been retained by the Chinese Benevolent Association.

Perhaps the most shocking and disturbing element of the whole trial took place just prior to Wong taking his place in the dock. Mr Alexander Henderson KC, prosecuting on behalf of the Scottish Societies, insisted that before

Wong gave any evidence, he must first take the 'Chicken Oath'. This, he explained to the bemused judge, was the most binding of all Chinese oaths. The performance of the ritual was described to Scottish readers by the *Sunday Post* as follows:

It was a weird ceremony, performed on a field outside the Court, and consisted of reading a statement printed on a yellow piece of paper which, translated into English, means "that, provided he told the truth, he and his children and all descendants would enjoy prosperity and win the pleasures of heaven. If he did not, then might he die in the streets and might a similar fate befall his dear ones." The paper was then burned, and Wong was handed a cleaver, with which he cut off the head of a chicken to sanctify the oath.

Wong then took his place in the witness box and categorically denied the suggestion put to him by the prosecution that he had killed Janet Smith as an act of revenge when she had refused his advances. He explained the blood on his apron by telling the court that he lifted the dead girl's head, on finding the body. He also denied ever making any improper suggestions towards her, telling the court that he had 'always been kind to her.'

Although at the original inquest (and subsequently in newspapers) it was widely stated that Wong had given Janet Smith a gift of 'a nightie and a camisole', it was not reported until much later that such gifts were, in fact, common among devoted Chinese servants. Wong Foon Sing and the Bakers satisfied the court as to their movements on the day of Janet Smith's death, and the evidence that her body had been redressed after death added further doubt to Wong's guilt. An implication that Janet Smith had been involved in drug taking (due to a strange mark on her finger, often found on cocaine users) was refuted; and could not be proved one way or the other. Similarly, any suggestion of rape (or 'ravishment' as it was referred to during the 1920s) could not be proved by the coroner, due to the damage caused by the embalming process.

For the first time it was made public that Janet Smith had a sweetheart, Arthur Dawson, from Robert's Creek in British Columbia, who revealed that the couple had planned to marry and that she had never mentioned any doubts about Wong Foon Sing to him, nor had she (to be best of his knowledge) ever handled a gun.

As the trial progressed it became obvious that not a shred of evidence existed to incriminate Wong and finally, in October 1925, the case was thrown out of court.

Three of his kidnappers were imprisoned for their role in the plot to abduct and torture Wong but others, including Point Grey Police Chief John Murdoch, were acquitted. Murdoch was a former sergeant in the Glasgow City Police. The arrested kidnappers all proved to be police officers involved in the case, members of the Scottish Societies and the editor of a local newspaper. Wong had been able to identify the house in which they had imprisoned him for six weeks. On examination of the house, the floors revealed holes through which chains were placed to hold Wong captive and an improvised scaffold, from which the abductors hanged him in a last-ditch attempt to extract a confession. The revelation of the plot against Wong and his subsequent torture by well-known members of the Vancouver Police sent shockwaves through Canadian society.

Following his release from custody Wong (understandably) returned to China, and despite the offer of a $3,000 reward by the Chinese Council of Vancouver for information in the killing of Janet Smith, the investigation fizzled out. The police had no further suspects or made little effort to find one. The case remains unsolved to this day.

One of the more popular conspiracy theories that persists in Vancouver, even today, is that Janet Smith actually met her demise at a party held at 3851 Osler Avenue the night before her body was found. Various accounts described a drunken party and drug-fuelled orgy. In author Edward Starkins' 1984 book *Who Killed Janet Smith* he described meeting an elderly woman who recounted to him a death bed confession made several years earlier by Jack Nichol (son of former *Daily Province* publisher and lieutenant governor Walter Nichol).

Jack Nichol stated that he had attended the party at 3851 Osler Avenue on the night of 25th July 1924. At the time he had been romantically involved with a girlfriend, who caught him *in flagrante* with Janet Smith in the bathroom and exploded with jealousy. During the affray that followed, Jack Nichol accidently knocked Janet Smith down, smashing her head on a spigot, killing her instantly. Her dead body was then dressed and, the following morning, staged to appear like a suicide or accident using the .45 revolver owned and kept by Mr Baker at his house. If this version of events is true, it also implies pre-existing knowledge of the Baker's gun. Whether the guilty parties assumed that Wong Foon Sing would then be blamed is not known. Jack Nichol died soon after this 'confession' and was never charged.

This account was also famously put forward by a self-proclaimed clairvoyant, Barbara Oxford, who variously claimed to have attended the same party, both in the flesh and in her visions. So much importance was placed upon her version of events that newspaper reporters successfully managed to sneak her into the house at 3851 Osler Ave, in order that she sense the real happenings on that night. She was shown one of the bedrooms, in which she claimed to have seen bloodstains during a vision, and an object was also stolen from the murder scene to help her contact the spirit of Janet Smith. Barbara Oxford also claimed that there was a bullet hole in the floor of the bedroom, the room in which she felt the murder had really taken place. Although taken seriously by the newspapers, this claim does not seem to have been investigated by the police. Interest in spiritualism and the occult was widespread in the years following the Great War. Many respected and prominent figures in society, including fellow Scot Sir Arthur Conan Doyle, had formed 'scientific' societies, dedicated to understanding the phenomenon, and any 'evidence' from clairvoyants was considered important.

Unknown in Canada at the time, was a story circulated in the *Dundee Courier* in September 1924 claiming that

Arthur Smith (Janet's father) had received three warnings in the form of visions during the three nights prior to his daughter's death. He claimed to have seen his daughter struggling for help, surrounded by shadowy figures. The dreams were so remarkable and clear they became imprinted on his mind.

Frederick Baker insisted there was no party of any kind that night at Osler Avenue. He twice sued the Vancouver newspapers, denying their claims that he was involved in drug trafficking or the like. However, Baker was, as Scotland Yard records would later reveal, an international drug smuggler; a point which was not known at the time.

Interestingly, during my research for this story I came across two contradictory pieces of evidence given by Frederick Baker at Wong's trial. The significance of these two points seems to have rather been missed at the time. After all, Baker was not on trial; and the natural deference at the time towards wealthy members of high society ensured that his cross examination was not particularly vigorous. Firstly, when questioned about the discovery of Janet's body on the day of the murder, Baker claimed in court that her body had 'straightened out', or 'stiffened'. *Rigor Mortis* would not set in until several hours after death and could not have occurred if Janet Smith had only just died.

Was this a slip by Baker? It certainly was not followed up. Secondly, he later claimed that when he first saw the body on the floor of the laundry room, blood was still pouring from the wound on the side of Janet's head. This was refuted by Dr Blackwood (the first doctor at the scene), who claimed the blood was already matted in her hair. Was this a clumsy attempt by Baker to make it appear as if the shooting had only just taken place? Both points seem at odds with the official version of events, yet neither was investigated further.

The death of Janet Smith, whether by suicide, accident, or murder, remains unsolved. The case raised huge and significant public debate in Canada; yet is almost completely unknown in the city of Janet Smith's birth. The mystery was not mere tabloid fodder but, rather, social drama that led Vancouverites to ask complex and uncomfortable questions about their city, province, and attitudes to race. The various Chinese Associations in Vancouver protested vigorously about the treatment of Wong, but in 1920s Vancouver their voice was not heard or listened to.

Janet Smith's headstone at Mountain View Cemetery in Vancouver was purchased by the United Council of Scottish Societies, partly funded by money raised in Perth.

Even today, it is still rumoured in Vancouver that the ghostly figure of Janet Smith haunts the lush, tree-lined avenues of Shaughnessy

Heights. A century after her death the story is told nightly to fascinated tourists on the city's famous 'Ghost Tours'.

Following the completion of the trial the Scottish *Sunday Post* published an interview with Arthur Smith and extracts of Janet's last letter home to her parents, received just two days before her death:

> *I am very happy, my only regret is that I am bit far away from home. But never mind, early next year, mum, I shall have enough for a holiday. Just you and me mum. You'll love Canada.*

THE CHAMPAGNE
(AND FALSE TEETH) LIFESTYLE

John Frederick Bain Weir was blessed with an unusually furtive imagination, perhaps inherited from his American father who had sailed the world. John Weir was intelligent, had a pleasant manner, and the ability to charm his way into, and out of, any situation. So confident was he in his own capabilities that he frequently conducted his own defence in court (sometimes summing up for over an hour), spinning yarns that ranged from the sublime to the ridiculous. Indeed, it became almost impossible to separate the truth from the fiction.

With a staggering number of aliases, or variations on his name, John Weir strode confidently into shops, businesses and lodging houses under the pseudonyms John, Alexander, James, and Bain, or using the surnames McPherson, Weir, Scott, Paterson, or Hamilton.

Weir was released from Perth Prison in early December 1927, after having served a 12-month sentence for fraud. It had been his 36th conviction for obtaining money under false pretences, all in a six-year period since 1921. Weir had received prison sentences in all 36 cases and had been incarcerated for periods ranging from one week to eighteen months. He was still only 33 years of age.

Winter had arrived early in 1927. By the beginning of December, the streets of Perth were already icy and the temperatures frigid. The country was hit by intense blizzards and in London alone, 1,600 people were hospitalised after falling in the treacherous conditions.

Work was hard to come by too, as queues at the labour exchanges in Scotland were beginning to lengthen. Fuel was in short supply and the government had just nationalised the coal industry in an effort to increase production. Life for the average working man in Scotland was hard; for what seemed like little financial reward or security.

John Weir, however, had no intention of securing gainful employment, of working hard, or of suffering from the cold.

Just one week after being released from Perth Prison on 14th December, Weir casually walked into Robertson's the Jewellers in High Street, Leven, in Fife. He spoke to Mr Robertson, the shopkeeper, and inquired about purchasing a watch as a present for his father, Mr Paterson, a local dairyman. Because Mr Paterson was known to the shopkeeper, he agreed to let Weir take the watch in order that he could show his father. Weir then promised to return with payment for the watch as soon as he had been paid. The shopkeeper, who was completely taken in by Weir's plausible and pleasant manner, was staggered – just two days later – when he passed Mr Paterson, the dairyman, in the street. On inquiring if Mr Paterson liked his new watch, he was shocked to learn that the dairyman had not received any new watch, nor did he have a son!

The matter was reported to the police, who recognised the shopkeeper's description of Weir. He was arrested soon afterwards and appeared in Perth Sheriff's Court on 9th January 1928. With 36 previous convictions, Weir was never likely to succeed with a plea of not guilty, so instead threw himself on the mercy of the court with an elaborate tale of woe. This time Weir chose not to speak in his own defence, instead speaking through his defence solicitor, Mr JAG Hunter. An intricate story of Weir's past was laid before the court. It was claimed that Weir:

Was an intelligent and qualified man, who had held the position of Depute Inspector of Mines. Unfortunately, during the Great War, he had suffered the effects of mustard gas, as well as shell shock from an explosion. Since 1921, Mr Hunter informed the court, *Weir has been confined in various mental institutions in Scotland. Indeed Mr Weir was, in fact, only released from the mental ward of Edinburgh Infirmary on the understanding that his sister, Rosemary, would care for him.*

Rosemary was next to speak, she then informed the court that, on the day of the offence, Weir had met some old army acquaintances and was 'much the worse for drink' when he had visited Robertson's Jewellers in Leven. Weir, himself, then claimed he could not even remember the incident.

Mr MJ Howman, the Procurator Fiscal for Perthshire, and Sheriff Valentine were not impressed with Weir's defence claims, however. Howman told the court:

There has never been any suggestion that there was anything mentally wrong with the accused, and the procedure he has adopted in this case does not suggest it.

Sheriff Valentine remarked to the court that he could not remember seeing an accused man with so many convictions before and there did not appear to be any truth in his claims. Weir was sentenced to three months imprisonment.

Early in 1930 Weir found himself in trouble again, this time in Edinburgh Sheriff's Court, on a charge of obtaining money by fraudulent means, in the Musselburgh district of the city. Weir managed to have the proceedings deferred, and admitted himself into Perth Infirmary, claiming that he was suffering from both mental illness and tuberculosis. An examination was ordered. Unfortunately for Weir, the doctor's opinion, did not seem to assist his case:

Weir is not tubercular, and is not mentally deranged. In my opinion he is doing his best to escape prison.

Weir did not succeed. He was sentenced to a further six months at His Majesty's Pleasure.

His claims of chronic tuberculosis continued well into 1931, at which point he was sentenced to six months imprisonment at Cupar Sheriff's Court – this time on five counts of fraud. On this occasion. Weir had claimed he was a linesman for the General Post Office and desperately needed money for his bus fare home. He managed to convince five separate women that he was a friend of their husbands and obtained one shilling, from each of them, for his troubles. Whilst the amounts involved were not huge, his by now 45 previous convictions no doubt helped Sheriff Honeyman's decision to impose a far longer sentence than would usually be applied. Weir, on hearing the sentence, addressed the court, stating:

I am a chronic tubercular case, with only a short time to live, and do care very much what happens to me!

Despite Weir's protestations of his imminent departure from this life, he was fully engaged again in his nefarious activities by the early part of 1933. On 22nd February he knocked on the door of a house in Bridge Street, Comrie, near Crieff, and asked the occupant, Mrs Frost, if she was able to help an old soldier, down on his luck. Weir claimed to have just been discharged from Stracathro Military Hospital in Angus. He embellished his tale of woe even further by claiming that the doctor at the military hospital had ordered Weir to claim his full military pension of £400 immediately, rather than the customary weekly allowance of 12 shillings. This, Weir informed Mrs Frost, would necessitate a delay of ten months until at least December. He intended to buy a motor car with the money but, in the meantime, he had to support a wife and child at his lodging in South Street, Perth. His plausibility was enough to induce Mrs Frost to part with £6 (approximately £400 today).

A month later Weir walked into a solicitor's office in Oban, claiming to be the cousin of the senior partner. He informed the staff that one of the senior partners in the practice had promised to loan him 32 shillings to help with his financial difficulties. The claim was not believed, and the Oban Police were called while a clerk kept Weir talking. He was arrested immediately.

Once again, Weir appeared at Perth Sheriff's Court and was sentenced to six months' imprisonment by Sheriff Valentine.

1934 was a busy year for Weir. In April, he once again found himself in front of Sheriff Valentine at Perth Sheriff's Court. This time, facing no less than seven counts of fraud. The charges were read to the packed courthouse:

At the beginning of the year – in January and February – of (1) the sum of £2 from the Coupar Angus Ex-Servicemen's Association: (2) board and lodgings valued at 21s 5d from Mrs Burns 94 High Street, Perth; (3) and (4) board and lodging valued at 32s 2d, and 2s of money, from Mrs Cunningham, 14 Commercial Street, Bridgend, Perth; (5) a complete set of dentures to the value of £10 from the dental surgery at 3 Princes Street, Perth, occupied by Hugo & Victoria Liebow; (6) a bottle of champagne, value 13s 2d, from Messrs RB Smith & Sons, wine merchants, John Street, Perth; and (7) a half bottle of whisky, value 6s 3d, from the same firm.

It can only be presumed that Weir required some false teeth for himself, as a set of tailor-made dentures would surely be a rather difficult item to sell to someone else!

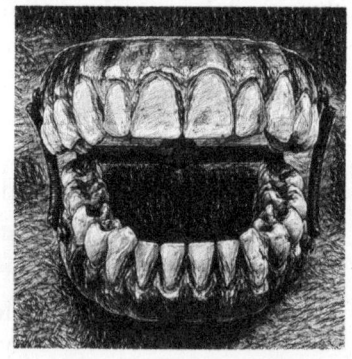

Weir pleaded not guilty to all charges and began his own

defence, producing, perhaps, his most elaborate story yet. He claimed that he had been employed as a spy for the Canadian secret service during the great war and was in receipt of a Canadian government war pension. To obtain the board and lodgings, the false teeth, and the champagne, he had simply made out a written account for the items in question, placed it in an envelope, and made an elaborate show of addressing the letter to The High Commissioner for Canada, Canada House, London. He then assured his victim that they 'would receive full satisfaction for their account directly from the High Commissioner of Canada'

When the Canadian High Commission refused to pay the accounts, Weir then claimed he had studied for a degree in agriculture, at British Columbia University and had been offered employment at the Department of Agriculture, who would in turn bring his outstanding bills up to date.

Mr Clark, prosecuting, retorted 'Mr Weir, your whole story is a parcel of lies – from beginning to end!'.

Sheriff Valentine, unimpressed with Weir's one hour summing up, sentenced him to a further three months in prison. The false teeth (as stolen goods) were returned to the dentists, Hugo & Liebow, leaving Weir, quite literally, speechless with rage!

In 1936 Weir attempted a second bite of the cherry; and this time received a larger sentence as his reward. Under the name Frederick Bain Weir, he called on a Leith public house, claiming to be a representative of a hotel in the Borders. Once he had gained the confidence of the hotel's owner, he offered the owner £8,000 for the purchase of the establishment. He then managed to obtain the sum of £1 from the owner of the public house, £3 from the taxi driver (who had driven him there), and a similar sum (for a similar ruse) from another hotel in Galashiels. Sheriff-Principal Brown, at Edinburgh Sheriff's Court found Weir guilty and sentenced him to 12 months' imprisonment. Needless to say, Weir once again pled not guilty to all the charges.

The Second World War arrived in 1939 and Weir, although still only 45 years of age, managed to escape any form of conscription into the army. Perhaps he felt that jail was the safest place to sit out the hostilities, since he appears to have spent the majority of the conflict incarcerated in Perth Prison?

Following the war, however, he found himself in trouble once again. In April 1947 he admitted three charges of fraud at Edinburgh Sheriff's Court. Weir had persuaded an 82- year-old woman to loan him £22 15s, in order (he claimed) that he could travel to London to receive £750 in compensation for the death of his sons during the conflict. He then told the old lady that his wife had died, and that he needed £10 to pay for her burial in Montrose, and a further £10 to enable him to purchase another set of dentures. Sheriff MacDonald sentenced Weir to a further 12 months incarceration, describing him as 'a regular trickster, who makes his living by fraud.'

Once in prison, Weir managed to convince his cellmate, a naïve 20-year-old named Kenneth Brown, to take part in a string of burglaries upon their release. In January 1948 the pair broke into four separate draper's shops in Perth, Leven, Kirkcaldy, and Burntisland, stealing articles worth £130. Weir was returned straight back to prison for a further six months.

Weir's largest fraud, however, seems to have been his last, and the crime for which he received his longest sentence. In September 1948 he appeared at Edinburgh Sheriff's Court on 31 charges of obtaining money by deception from two elderly ladies in Perth, whom it appears he had befriended. Managing to convince the two old women (who were aged 60 and 77 respectively) that he was due to collect £750 from a Colonel in the Black Watch that he had helped during the war. He managed to persuade the two elderly ladies to part with £274, in a series of transactions, before their suspicions were finally aroused.

On this occasion Weir pleaded guilty and asked for 12 previous offences to be taken into account. Despite claiming that his life was nearly at an end due to bronchitis, Weir received a sentence of two years in prison – his largest single stretch.

By the time of his release in 1950 Weir was 69 years of age. He does not appear to have crossed paths with the law again. In fact, he seems to have disappeared altogether. Perhaps he retired, or maybe Weir finally relented from his life of crime? Did he finally succumb to one of the many ailments he claimed to have, or did he eventually manage to take his revenge on the system that he alleged, 'has always had one over on me, but I'll get my one big score one of these days.'

During his many incarcerations, Weir was frequently overheard boasting to his cellmates, that the police would never catch him again.

Perhaps the only crumb of comfort for John Weir, on release from prison, would have been the formation of the National Health Service in 1948, allowing him access to a free set of dentures for the first time!

THE BLAIRGOWRIE MURDER

The mood in Scotland was a sombre one in the winter of 1971. Cold and unpleasant conditions gripped the country. Sixty Six spectators had recently been killed in a stairway crush at the New Year Rangers v Celtic football match and three young Scottish soldiers had been lured from a bar in Belfast and shot by the Provisional Irish Republican Army during the Northern Ireland troubles.

In Blairgowrie, life continued as normal in that depressing post-Christmas lull. Most of the hotels and restaurants were now entering the quiet period that follows the festivities. However, the Muirton House Hotel, a large red stone Victorian building on the Perth Road, had been unusually busy on the evening of Sunday 10th January 1971. A large, private party had taken place in the hotel's function room that night. James Keltie, the hotel's owner, as well as overseeing the event, had earlier been forced to refuse entry to a rowdy group of youths who had tried to gate-crash the gathering.

Finally, late in the evening, the guests had at last dispersed, none of them choosing to spend the night at the hotel. At around midnight Mr Keltie, aged 52, decided to retire to his bedroom. He kissed his wife Agnes goodnight, and went to a different bedroom, at the far end of the building. It appears that relations between the couple were rocky, and they had slept in separate rooms for some time.

Meanwhile, despite the late hour, a car sat idling on the roadside close to the hotel.

Sometime in the early hours of the morning, a man (or possibly two men) managed to gain entry into the hotel, through an unalarmed sash window on the ground floor. The man (or men) carefully manoeuvred the catch that secured the window frame to one side with a long knife, and then pushed the window silently upwards. Once inside they cut the hotel's telephone line and quietly made their way up the staircase towards James Keltie's room. They seemed to know exactly which bedroom was Mr Keltie's, as they made little noise and did not disturb Mrs Keltie from her slumber, nor wake any of their three children, who were also asleep in other bedrooms. After silently entering the room the men grabbed James Keltie, before he could react, and stripped his night clothes from him, gagging him so he could not yell out. Once the terrified Mr Keltie had been subdued, his hands and feet were tightly bound and he was dragged or carried from his bed, across the room, down the stairs and outside into the hotel garage. The horrific chain of events seems to have been accomplished at lightning speed and with silent, deadly efficiency.

Once outside the hotel and knowing that they could not be overheard from the main building, the man (or men) produced an iron wrench, which had been concealed underneath his jacket, and beat Keltie savagely, fracturing his skull and causing massive bleeding. His attackers left him for dead, first stopping to steal some whisky from the hotel (but no cash, despite the takings from the previous evening's party still being on the premises), before making their escape silently from the hotel, tossing the bloodied wrench into a nearby field as he, or they, made their getaway.

Mrs Keltie was not disturbed by the events of the night and was still asleep at 8am the following morning when a local taxi driver discovered Mr Keltie's body. The taxi driver was regularly employed to take the Keltie's three children, aged 5, 9 and 16, to school. The early mornings were usually a busy time at the hotel, so the taxi firm was often employed to pick up the children. Whilst waiting outside the hotel for the children to emerge the taxi driver, noticing the open garage door, made the grim discovery. Incredibly James Keltie was still alive despite the terrible injuries he had suffered. An ambulance and the police were called. However, Mr Keltie died from massive internal bleeding before he could reach Dundee Royal Infirmary.

The police immediately launched a massive murder investigation, the largest in Perthshire's history. Over 100 officers were drafted in from across Scotland and Chief

Inspector John (Jock) Lamond of Perth CID took charge of the operation. Door to door inquiries were made at every house in Blairgowrie, all outlying communities, and for a seven mile stretch along the road to Coupar Angus. Every householder in the town was questioned. Extra officers brought in from the Angus Constabulary assisted and a painstaking search was made of the hotel grounds and nearby fields. With the huge number of officers employed on the case, an early breakthrough seemed likely. Indeed, several clues were forthcoming, including the discovery of the blood-stained wrench in a nearby field. In addition, a handful of witnesses reported seeing a man close to the hotel at approximately 4am on the morning of the 11th January. The timeline seemed to fit with the suspected time of the attack and an appeal was immediately issued to locate the man.

The following description was given to the local press and an urgent plea made for the man to come forward:

Perthshire Police are looking for a man, aged 26-28, wearing a khaki jacket seen walking near the hotel at 4.40am on the morning of the attack.

The man was never traced or identified, nor did anyone matching the description ever make themselves known to the investigation team.

Following the discovery of the wrench in a nearby field, and some discarded whisky bottles, police immediately settled on robbery as a motive, possibly by someone with local knowledge. Had someone known that a large party was due to take place in the hotel on that evening, and expected to find large amounts of cash on the premises? Was James Keltie beaten savagely, in order that he would disclose the location of the night's takings, only for the intruders to then panic thinking they had killed him before he was able to reveal the hiding place? This theory would account for the fact that only whisky had been stolen from the hotel. Witnesses had also reported seeing an Austin 1100 at around 5am, travelling from Blairgowrie to Perth. The car was cream or white in colour and appeared to have two occupants. This sighting did match the timeline; but was otherwise vague.

Next, an attempt was also made to trace the four youths who had unsuccessfully attempted to gate-crash the private function at the hotel during the earlier part of the evening. It was thought, perhaps, they had a score to settle with Mr Keltie and had later broken into the hotel as a form of revenge. However, the youths could not be traced. Seemingly, Mr Keltie had been the only witness who had seen them properly. With no concrete leads to their identity, this line of inquiry was also eventually dropped.

Meanwhile, the hotel was dusted for fingerprints, which only revealed some partial results. Unfortunately, these 'partials' could not be matched to anything in the police files. As a result, DCI Lamond initiated one of the most ambitious (and expensive) lines of inquiry ever undertaken by Perthshire Police. It was decided to fingerprint every male over the age of 16 from Blairgowrie, Alyth, Coupar Angus and all surrounding villages. A special mobile unit was brought into Blairgowrie, at the request of DCI Lamond, to cope with the huge task. This time-consuming operation took several days with over 2,000 sets of fingerprints being taken in all. But, even after being further extended to outlying communities, the operation produced no matches for any of the partial fingerprints found at the scene.

The appeal for information about the Austin 1100 motor car, seen driving on the Blairgowrie to Perth road, during the early morning of 11th January, proved to be unconnected, as did the car seen parked on the roadside near the hotel, late on the Sunday evening. The occupants of both vehicles were eliminated from the police's inquiries.

Next, the police, still convinced that robbery was the motive, switched to the *modus operandi* of the crime itself. After contacting other forces, the style seemed to match that of a serial offender known to police in England. Officers travelled to the Midlands to question the man. Unfortunately, this line of enquiry also proved fruitless, the man had the perfect alibi – he had been in hospital at the time of the attack on Mr Keltie.

Despite all the seemingly positive leads drawing a blank, DCI Lamond did not give up. Perth Police continued house to house inquiries, but with no success. The Provost of Blairgowrie, Mr James Drennan-Smith, made one last, heartfelt plea to the residents of the town:

The murder of Mr Keltie in such a brutal way is quite the worst crime to be committed in Perthshire this century. In order that the person or persons who committed this dastardly crime can be brought to justice, I appeal to every citizen to co-operate with the police in their inquiries.

Two weeks after the murder, on a dismal day in late January, James Keltie's funeral was held in Blairgowrie. A large crowd lined the procession route to the cemetery and plain clothed police officers mingled with the crowd and the mourners, in the hope that the killer might be among them. This line of enquiry also proved fruitless, the police noting that no individual's behaviour seemed to be out of the ordinary, or in any way peculiar.

Inevitably, as time passed, the investigation was scaled back, first to 20 officers, then eventually – with all avenues apparently explored and no fresh leads - the file became a 'cold case'. Yet, despite this scaling down, questions were asked, and rumours remained rife locally. It seems that James Keltie had not been a popular man; and many had questioned his business dealings. Had he upset a business rival? Was his murder actually an act of revenge, dressed up to appear as a botched robbery?

Police officer Willie MacFarlane took up a posting at Blairgowrie in 1974, three years after the murder, and became fascinated with the unsolved case. It seemed to him that other lines of inquiry should have been followed up more ruthlessly. Was the vicious attack on Mr Keltie merely revenge from the four youths who had been refused admittance to the hotel on the night of the attack? Could more effort have been made to identify the four young troublemakers? After all, identifying a group of four friends, in such a small community, could surely be achieved?

Although a robbery gone wrong was originally thought to

be the motive, PC Willie MacFarlane was never convinced. The level of violence and the time taken over the attack did not seem to fit with a burglar caught in the act. Surely, in such a scenario, the offender would have just made a quick getaway. The question of the untouched hotel takings did not fit with the theory of a robbery either. If the burglars had time to steal whisky, they certainly had time to take cash. After all, why go to such desperate lengths to find the location of the money and then not take it? Or why not simply conduct a search for the takings first, and then resort to a violent attack only as a last recourse? Nothing seemed to make sense.

Members of James Keltie's own family were convinced bitter business rivals were behind the crime. His niece Jean, who was 28 at the time of the murder, said;

He was a very successful businessman, but he perhaps took short-cuts to get where he did. Maybe that's why something happened. Perhaps he made enemies in the business world. I am sure he must have had some dodgy dealings going on.

James Keltie's wife Agnes, with whom he had a difficult relationship, was also questioned. Why had she not overheard the attack? Why did she not raise the alarm in the morning? She was also unpopular with the rest of the family. However, Agnes was a retired police officer and investigators were convinced she was not involved in the attack.

Another theory put forward was that Agnes had somehow incurred the wrath of a criminal gang in Perthshire, during her time as a police officer? Had the killing been some sort of underworld retribution? However, there seemed to be little evidence to support the theory at the time and this avenue of enquiry was not given serious consideration by the investigating officers.

After retirement in 2010, still haunted by the unsolved case, Willie MacFarlane decided to dedicate a chapter in his book, *The History of the Perthshire and Kinross-shire Constabularies*, to the mystery.

To me, he said, *it seems that the original inquiry team just lost momentum. They focused on a man out walking at 4am and also a known criminal, who had been in hospital at the time. They came up with several theories, but they all died a death — so was someone brought in to do an inside job? I have been interested in this case my whole career and would like to see it solved before I end up in the police station in the sky. When I was a young cop, I always got the feeling that people out there did know and would not come forward.*

As a result of renewed interest in the murder Tayside Police reviewed the cold case in 2011, however, no new lines of inquiry or fresh clues came to light. Despite the biggest investigation in the history of policing in Perthshire, no one has ever been brought to justice for the brutal murder of James Keltie and the case remains unsolved. Ex-PC Willie MacFarlane maintained that someone in Blairgowrie knew something but did not come forward.

James Keltie was buried in Blairgowrie cemetery. His wife Agnes died four years later. The Muirton House Hotel was sold immediately after the horrific murder and continued to operate as a hotel for several years before eventually becoming a nursing home.

THE BUTLER DID IT

During December of 1977, as Yorkshire police appealed for help in the hunt for Peter Sutcliffe, the 'Yorkshire Ripper', an unlikely party of four people checked into the Bridge of Tilt Hotel at Blair Atholl in Perthshire. Two younger men, a much older man, who appeared quite out of sorts, and a middle-aged woman wearing a wig, expensive jewellery, and a mink coat. Their behaviour was odd and more conspicuous than the usual visitors, especially as it was now out of season, and the hotel was virtually empty.

The following morning the strange group of four went out for the day, returning later that evening. They offered no explanation, spoke to no one, and checked out the next day. They returned again a few days later, this time without the older gentleman, stayed the night, then left early the following morning.

One of the two younger men in the group of four at the Bridge of Tilt Hotel that December was later identified as Archibald Hall. In December 1977 he was midway through a killing spree that would see him become one of Britain's most notorious serial killers. However, the chain of events, leading up to the tragedies of December 1977 and January 1978, had begun several years earlier.

Archibald Hall had been born in Glasgow, in 1924. His career in crime had started at the age of 15. Inevitably, by the time he reached 20, he had been sentenced for a string of petty offences, eventually being sent to prison. He served his first jail sentence for attempting to sell jewellery in London, which he had previously stolen in both Perth and Edinburgh. During his time behind bars, Hall studied antiques, the etiquette of the English aristocracy, as well as taking elocution lessons to soften his Scottish accent. Capitalising on the profits of his criminal ventures, he was then able to move to London where he found himself able to mix in a wide range of social circles. He was able to converse in perfect upper-class English, even passing himself off as a Lord on occasion. In 1964, while working as a jewel thief, Archibald Hall was caught red-handed and ended up in prison once more. This time he was sentenced to ten years. However, he escaped, was recaptured, and then returned to prison – with a further five years added to his sentence.

Following his release from prison, Archibald Hall began using the name Roy Fontaine, inspired by the actress Joan Fontaine, and managed to find employment as a butler, occasionally suffering further spells in jail, mainly for the theft of jewellery. He also married and divorced during this period and, once again, impersonated a Lord.

In 1975, Archibald Hall was released from prison once more and returned to Scotland. With false references, and again using the name Roy Fontaine, he obtained employment as butler to Lady Margaret ('Peggy') Hudson, a dowager (widow of Sir Austin Hudson, 1st Baronet, and a Conservative MP) at her family home, Kirtleton House in Dumfriesshire. Hall had initially planned to steal her valuables, but he never carried this plan out when he realised that he liked both his job and employer too much.

However, an unfortunate and chance encounter would act as a catalyst, leading to a truly horrific chain of events. When David Wright, an acquaintance from Hall's last prison term, was also given a job on the estate as a gamekeeper in 1977, there was immediate friction between the two men. Wright frequently begged and borrowed money from Hall, threatening to reveal to Lady Hudson that the pair had met in prison, if Hall refused to pay him.

Wright then stole a valuable ring belonging to Lady Hudson; however, Hall forced him to return it, claiming that he wanted to 'go straight'. That night, in retribution, after drinking six bottles of champagne between them, David Wright discharged a firearm as Hall slept. The bullet missed Hall, ending up in the headboard. The following day, Hall invited Wright to go out into the grounds of the estate on a rabbit shoot, on the pretext of talking their argument through and reaching an amicable solution. However, as Wright took pot-shots at the rabbits, Hall carefully counted the rounds as Wright gradually used up all his ammunition. When he was certain Wright could no longer defend himself, Hall shot him in the back of the head in an act of retribution and cold-hearted self-preservation. After burying Wright's body under boulders in a stream on the estate, he hurried back to the house. Up until that moment Hall had never committed an act of violence (having only been involved in offences of theft). From this point on, however, he would transform into one of Britain's most notorious serial killers, dubbed 'The Monster Butler'.

Hall then returned to work as normal. The absence of David Wright would eventually be noticed, but Hall felt sure it would just be assumed that Wright was an unreliable type and had simply moved on. Shortly after the killing, during a routine check with the police, Archibald Hall's true identity was revealed, and Lady Hudson immediately dismissed him from her service. Hall's brutal slaying of David Wright had been entirely pointless. Had he not taken Wright's life, perhaps the following inexorable chain of events may never have unfolded as they did.

Hall then decided to try his luck in London. Using his assumed name, Roy Fontaine, and thanks to his plausible nature and smart appearance he was able to secure employment as butler to the prosperous Scott-Elliot's. Walter Scott-Elliot was the retired Member of Parliament for Accrington and from a wealthy Scottish aristocratic family. Now aged 82 he had retired and settled in London with his glamorous wife Dorothy, aged 60.

Hall was given considerable latitude by the Scott-Elliots, who even presented him with blank, signed cheques to purchase essentials. However, Hall always intended to systematically rob them of their considerable collection of antiques and valuables, believing he had deceived them into trusting him completely.

On 8th December 1977 Hall met with a male accomplice, Michael Kitto, in a King's Cross pub and together they hatched a plan to defraud the Scott-Elliots. Believing that Mr Scott-Elliot would already be in bed asleep, and that Mrs Scott-Elliot had booked into a nursing home for a few days (to receive treatment for her arthritis), Hall took Kitto to their London flat to view the family's collection of antiques. However, they unexpectedly found Dorothy Scott-Elliot at home and in her bedroom. Unsurprisingly, she demanded to know exactly what Hall was doing, and who his accomplice was. An argument ensued and the pair knocked Mrs Scott-Elliot to the floor. A violent scuffle followed, and the pair were forced to cover Mrs Scott-Elliot's face with a pillow to stifle her screams. In doing so they suffocated her. Whether they had actually intended to kill her is doubtful, as they required her signature on blank cheques and forged documents to carry out their ongoing plan to systematically defraud the unfortunate couple. In any event, thinking quickly, they placed her in bed and arranged her body in a position that suggested she was asleep. When Mr Scott-Elliot appeared at the door, no doubt woken by the commotion, Hall explained that Mrs Scott-Elliot had screamed due to a nightmare and had gone back to sleep.

After managing to sedate the 82-year-old Walter Scott-Elliot with extra doses of his medication, Hall and Kitto knew they needed to conjure up a scheme to dispose of the body; enabling them to continue their plan to strip the property of its valuables.

Early the following morning, in King's Cross, Hall and Kitto met with a 51-year-old prostitute called Mary Coggle. Mary was a long-time acquaintance of Kitto's and a former housekeeper to the Scott-Elliots. Together they evolved a plan to pass Mary off as the late Mrs Scott-Elliot, hoping that her heavily medicated husband would believe her to be his wife. A car was rented (using a blank cheque signed by Mrs Scott-Elliot) and Mary Coggle, wearing a wig and sunglasses, and dressed in Mrs Scott-Elliot's mink coat and jewellery, sat in the back seat of the car with Mr Scott-Elliot. His wife's body had by this time been secreted in the boot of the car. The foursome, with the corpse still hidden in the boot and some looted valuables from the Scott-Elliot's home, then headed north. After calling overnight at a cottage in Cumbria, owned by Hall's family, they proceeded to Scotland. During the journey they managed to keep the 82-year-old Walter Scott-Elliot sedated and in a semiconscious state of confusion.

After booking into the Bridge of Tilt Hotel in Blair Atholl, in the north of Perthshire, the three criminals left Mr Scott-Elliot unconscious in the car, parked in the hotel car park, with his wife's body in the boot, while they drank in the hotel bar. If anyone enquired, they planned to explain that Mr Scott-Elliot was sleeping due to the long drive. The following morning the party left Blair Atholl and headed on the quiet country roads, via Aberfeldy, towards Crieff looking for a suitably quiet and secluded spot to dispose of the body. The ideal spot needed to be deserted, but not too far from the road due to the problems involved in carrying a body. Eventually they found an appropriate place for their purpose, by the side of a quiet B827 back road between the villages of Braco and Comrie in Perthshire. After first making sure they could not be observed by any passing traffic they hauled Mrs Scott-Elliot's body from the boot of the car and buried her close to the roadside.

The group then returned across country to the Bridge of Tilt Hotel for the night. After checking out the following morning, they headed northwest to the remote A831 road that skirts the bends in the River Glass through Strathglass in Glen Affric. At a secluded spot, approximately halfway between Inverness and the Kyle of Lochalsh, Hall and Kitto took Walter Scott-Ellis from the car and attempted to strangle him. However, the old man unexpectedly put up a spirited struggle, and Hall was forced to hit him over the head with the shovel that he had used to dig Mrs Scott-Elliot's grave on the previous day. Once they were certain that Mr Scott-Elliot was dead, the two men took the blood splattered shovel and disposed of his body in a shallow grave close to the water. Mary Coggle watched on, still wearing the mink coat.

After visiting Inverness and Aviemore, the three again returned to the Bridge of Tilt Hotel and spent a further night before checking out. They drove south towards Perth where they sold some of the Scott-Elliot's antiques. They then returned over the border to the cottage in Cumbria, which was owned by Hall's family. Hall knew it would only be a matter of time before the Scott-Elliots were reported missing; but didn't think the disappearance of David Wright would be noticed at Lady Hudson's estate, Kirkleton House. Wright had always been the unreliable sort, and hopefully Lady Hudson would assume he had just left. In the meantime, Hall wanted to keep as low a profile as possible while the group travelled back and forth to the Scott-Elliot's home in London, methodically stripping the flat of all its valuable antiques, and then returning to Edinburgh and Perth to sell them. Hall realised their party had been seen by hotel staff in several locations and would be remembered easily should the police enquire; therefore, it was essential to their plan to remain as incognito as possible.

Unfortunately, Mary Coggle had rather taken to wearing Mrs Scott-Ellis's mink coat and jewellery, even parading it around King's Cross when the group returned to London. Hall recognised that this was certain to draw attention to the group and instructed Mary to give up the mink coat. Mary flatly refused to take off the coat and flew into a violent rage. Sadly, at that moment, Mary signed her own death warrant. A huge argument erupted between the trio. Kitto held her down on the ground; and Hall beat her repeatedly with a poker in a frenzied act of revenge for her perceived disloyalty. Both men then suffocated her with a plastic bag. At daybreak the following morning they heaved her limp body into the boot of the car, drove across the border into Scotland and threw her corpse into a stream in Dumfriesshire.

The weeks slowly passed by, and everything seemed to be running smoothly for Hall and Kitto. Avoiding hotels whenever possible, Hall and Kitto stayed at the remote Cumbrian cottage, during which time they made several visits to the Scott-Elliot's apartment in London, stripping it bare.

Eventually, an antiques dealer became suspicious when two strangers offered him some valuable china and silverware at a price far below its market value. He jotted down the number plate of the car the men were driving and alerted the authorities. On checking, the police found the car had been rented in the name of Scott-Elliot and decided to visit the Scott-Elliot's Chelsea flat. Here they found the walls spattered with blood and over £3,500 worth of valuables missing (approximately £20,000 today)

Events reached a head in January of 1978, however. Hall's brother, Donald, had recently been released from prison and came to stay at the cottage. Hall loathed Donald for his coarseness and for what he perceived to be his brother's sexual perversions. Finally tensions between the pair reached breaking point. Following a heavy drinking session, Donald was tied up in the cottage, and a chloroform-soaked rag pressed into his face. He was then drowned in the bath. Surprisingly, despite chloroform's commonplace appearance in Hollywood films and crime novels, Donald Hall's death would become the first known 'chloroform murder' in Britain.

Hall decided they should be cautious and change vehicles. He rented a new Ford Granada and he and Michael Kitto hauled Donald Hall's body into the boot. Hall had first changed the registration plates of the car for false ones. Ironically, the Ford Granada had originally carried a '999' prefix, which Hall had taken an immediate dislike to. The two men headed north again to Perthshire, planning to bury the body of Donald Hall, in a similarly remote spot to that of his previous victims, this time somewhere in the hills between Crieff and Aberfeldy.

However, wintry weather had set in, making the roads treacherous, and the pair decided instead to check into the Blenheim House Hotel in North Berwick, close to Edinburgh. Had they been involved in a road accident due to the icy conditions in Perthshire, a body in the boot might have been difficult to explain! As Hall and Kitto drank in the hotel bar, the proprietor became suspicious – he thought the men seemed unlikely to pay their bill - and decided to telephone the police. On checking out the false registration number of the Granada, the officers discovered that the number actually belonged to a Ford Escort. Two police constables arrived at the hotel and, after examining the car in the hotel car park, found the two men eating dinner in the hotel bar. Unfortunately, for all his cunning and careful manoeuvring, Hall had omitted to change the tax disc on the car's windscreen, which still bore the original number, '999'. It was a relatively easy task to arrest the two men and they were immediately taken to the nearest police station for questioning on suspicion of stealing a car. The vehicle was also removed for examination.

On examination of the Ford Granada, the body of Donald Hall was discovered in the boot. With the matter now far more serious, the men were informed of their rights and were about to be handcuffed and locked in a cell when Hall asked to use the police station's toilet. The tenacious Hall then squeezed through the toilet window and fled. He hailed a lift from a local taxi driver, telling the driver that his wife had been in an accident but that he was unaware of the hospital she had been taken to. Whereupon he persuaded the taxi driver to drive him around for three hours, on the pretext of searching for the hospital, while the police searched in vain for their escaped prisoner. Finally, at a roadblock in Haddington, Hall was arrested again. Bizarrely, before being handcuffed, Hall insisted on paying the full taxi fare.

Hall tried and failed to commit suicide while in custody. When faced with the evidence from the owners of the Bridge of Tilt Hotel, who confirmed witnessing four people arriving and only three leaving the hotel, Hall admitted to three further murders. (He claimed Michael Kitto alone had killed Mrs Scott-Elliot). He then agreed to reveal the exact whereabouts of the three buried victims. In deep snow and bitter temperatures, and with the world's media watching, police teams dug up the bodies of David Wright at Kirkleton House, Walter Scott-Elliot from Glen Affric, and Dorothy Scott-Elliot from a roadside ditch near Braco.

He could not remember the location of his brother's body. The police charged Hall and Kitto with all five murders.

The cases were presented before courts on both sides of the border, due to the complicated geographical nature of the murders. Archibald Hall was convicted at court in both London and Edinburgh of four murders - the murder of Mrs Scott-Elliot was ordered to lie on file. He was sentenced to life imprisonment. In Scotland, it was recommended that he served a minimum of 15 years and in England the judge handed down a recommendation that he never be released. When passing sentence the judge added, 'Having regard to your cold-blooded behaviour and undoubted leadership in these dreadful matters, I recommend that you shall not be considered for parole during the rest of your natural life.'

Kitto was given life imprisonment for three murders, with no recommended minimum in Scotland and a 15-year minimum in England. Police said in evidence that Kitto was, in a perverted way, fortunate to be able to go on trial at all, as Hall had fully intended to kill him too.

Successive Home Secretaries put Hall on the list of dangerous prisoners who should serve a whole life tariff. Even when 'politically-set' tariffs were declared illegal by the Law Lords and the European Court of Human Rights, Hall's status as a prisoner 'unlikely to ever be released' was not altered, despite being the oldest prisoner on the publicised list. In 1995 *The Observer* newspaper published a letter from Hall in which he requested the right to die. He also attempted a hunger strike and made numerous suicide attempts, all of which were unsuccessful.

Hall published his autobiography, *A Perfect Gentleman*, in 1999 at the age of 75. He died of a stroke in Kingston Prison, Portsmouth, in 2002 at the age of 78. At that time of his death, he had become the oldest prisoner among the 70,000 held in British prisons.

But what transformed the likeable rogue and well-spoken butler into one of Britain's most ruthless killers? It had been hoped the question might have been explored in a film called *The Monster Butler*, produced by actor Malcolm McDowell, and starring Gary Oldman. However, despite production commencing in 2011, with extensive filming to take place in Perthshire, the movie was never completed, apparently due to financial constraints.

Perhaps the best clue to Archibald Hall's state of mind remains a chilling line from his biography in which he states: 'There is a side of me, when aroused, that is cold and completely heartless'.

THE BARON'S CHAUFFEUR

On Friday 14th April 1933 a smartly dressed young man exited from the Piccadilly Circus tube station in London and made his way upstairs into the spring sunshine. He folded his new underground map carefully, placed it in his inside jacket pocket, then, pausing only to light a cigarette, walked around the corner to the showrooms of the Daimler Motor Company.

Inside the showroom, with its curved glass windows and vaulted ceilings, strategically placed in front of several large potted plants were a handful of immaculately clean, prestige motor cars, aimed only at the most discerning customers. The young man glanced appreciatively at a black Daimler 25, a Humber Pullman, and a Sunbeam 20, among others, then turning to the salesman sat at his desk, he addressed him in a slight South African accent, 'I'd like to enquire about the hire of a motor car'.

Shown through to the manager's office, the young man introduced himself as Mr Edward Green, late of Cape Town in the colonies, and explained 'Good morning, sir. I have a money-making opportunity I would like to offer the garage.'

Having gained the manager's interest, Edward Green asked, 'if you would agree to lend me a suitable motor car for a few months, I will offer my services to potential travellers, as a chauffeur, and drive them on tours around the country.'

The manager of the garage, understandingly sceptical, was not quite sure how this arrangement could possibly benefit him. Green explained, 'I will telephone you or wire you once a week, from wherever I am in the country, and report how much money I have earned. I will then arrange to send half of my earnings back to you here at the garage and keep half for yourself.'

Green added, 'It will be far more profitable than simply allowing a car to sit idly in the showroom. Think of all those wealthy potential customers you have let slip through your hands. This way, we can all make some money. Everyone will benefit, sir, and no one will lose!'

He must have been a very persuasive individual indeed, as the manager of the garage readily agreed to Green's

dubious proposal – even allowing him to take the most luxurious model in the showroom (a six-cylinder Daimler 25 Limousine) when Green explained that the more luxurious the motor car, the higher a price he could charge!

Edward Green gave the owner a printed business card with his name and address on it and a deposit cheque for £25, drawn from a National Provincial Bank account. Contracts were duly signed, and the 32-year-old Edward Green drove away from the garage in a shiny new Daimler motor car. The address on the card proved to be false and the cheque, when presented at the bank, was returned to the garage, marked 'refer to drawer.' The proprietor of the garage would not see, or hear, from Edward Green again.

Green immediately picked up a friend, Harold Smith, who was waiting with their suitcases, and the pair headed speedily out of London along the Great North Road. The two men (of whom we can assume that their names were most likely aliases) had already devised an elaborate con trick. The expensive Daimler motor car was the final piece in their jigsaw. Edward Green was to pose as Baron Johan Willem Quarlos Van Ufford's chauffeur, his accomplice Harold as an employee of the Van Ufford household.

Surprisingly, the exotically sounding Baron Johan Willem Quarlos Van Ufford was a real person, and not a fictitious name dreamt up by Edward Green. The Van Ufford family had been members of the Dutch nobility for over 100 years. Originally of English descent, they were well known in society circles in both countries. Baron Johan Willem

Quarlos Van Ufford was the Queen's Commissioner and maintained a large house in London. During the spring and summer months he enjoyed the London 'season' and rarely left the capital.

Seemingly knowing that the Baron would not be leaving London during April and May, Edward Green and Harold Smith travelled throughout Britain and Ireland; booking luxurious hotel rooms in the name of the Baron, safe in the knowledge that he never left London at that time of year. On arrival at their chosen hotel, the pair would grandly inform the manager that Baron Quarlos Van Ufford intended to stay at the hotel; and would be arriving within the next day or so. Green explained that he had been sent ahead to assess the suitability of the rooms. In the meantime, he explained, any expenses for accommodation and food, which might be incurred, should be added to the Baron's account. This bill would be settled as soon as Baron Van Ufford arrived, Green assured the hotel. During their journey around the country any garage and fuel expenses were dealt with in a similar way. Sometimes, their deception might not raise the suspicions of the hotel's staff for several days,;sometimes the truth would be uncovered as early as the following morning, in which event they would claim that they were just on their way to collect the Baron from the local railway station. The pair would then leave the hotel, telling the management that they would return immediately with the Baron and settle any outstanding bill. They, of course, never returned.

Within two weeks the London showroom proprietor had reported the Daimler 25 motor car missing to the police, explained the circumstances, and given the detectives a description of Edward Green. The authorities agreed to keep a lookout for him and to return the motor car, if they were able to trace it. Not entirely certain of Green's intentions for the car, nor in which direction he had travelled, they wired a large number of regional police stations with descriptions of the car and the suspect. They also contacted several large and well-known hotels throughout the country, hoping that Green would appear at one of them. He did not. In fact, Edward Green had already been arrested.

A sharp-witted hotel receptionist in the Lake District had suspected Green and contacted the local police, who arrived quickly at the hotel. He was arrested before he could make his escape and charged with deception for which he spent two weeks in jail. Importantly, however, his arrest had occurred just before the description of the car had been circulated, and when Green emerged from his two-week incarceration the Daimler 25 was still parked in the same place that Green had left it. His accomplice, who had managed to avoid capture, had long since departed, leaving Green alone with the motor car, which had not, at that point, attracted any suspicion. Green had no idea where Harold Smith had fled to, nor any way of contacting him. Edward Green was now firmly on his own.

He was now presented with a simple choice. Either drive back to London, return the motor car, plead guilty and hope for a lenient sentence, or head further north and prolong his subsidised jaunt around the country. He chose the latter.

Deciding that he might be less likely to be detected the further north he travelled, he headed across the border into Scotland. The idea might well have been suggested to him by the astonishing reports that had received wall-to-wall coverage in all the nation's newspapers at the beginning of May. The sensational first photograph of the Loch Ness Monster had appeared widely and seemed to provide final proof of the existence of the monster. As a result, the narrow roads and rural hotels of Scotland were choked with tourists, all heading to Scotland in the hope of catching a glimpse of 'Nessie'. Perhaps Edward Green hoped that there would be safety in numbers. The roads and hotels of Scotland had never witnessed so many motor cars at once.

On Tuesday 30th May 1933 Edward Green drove up the impressive winding roadway leading to the Atholl Palace Hotel in Pitlochry. He entered the palatial reception area and asked to book suitable rooms in the name of Baron Johan Willem Quarlos Van Ufford. Green explained that Baron Van Ufford would be arriving in a couple of days and that, as the Baron's chauffeur, he had been sent ahead to secure accommodation. Green even expressed faux surprise when the hotel staff informed him that they had not yet received the Baron's letter of confirmation. Green assured them that the letter would arrive with the morning post.

Once adequately rested and refreshed, Green returned downstairs and asked the hotel staff if they could recommend a suitable local garage. The staff did so, and Green told them that he needed to take the motor car there for some essential repairs and would return shortly.

He called into the West End Garage in Pitlochry and spoke to the proprietor Mr George Watson. Green informed George Watson that Baron Van Ufford would be visiting Pitlochry, on the following day, and that the garage was to carry out all necessary repairs, servicing and refuelling of the motor car on behalf of the Baron. George Watson agreed; but told Green that the car would not be ready until the next morning and that he would require payment before the car could be released. Green agreed, stating that he had in his possession a signed cheque, in the name of Baron Van Ufford, ready to give the garage.

As requested, Green returned to the West End Garage the following morning and paid George Watson with a cheque apparently signed by Baron Van Ufford. The total bill for the servicing, spares, oil, and petrol was £13 6s 3d (approximately £925 today). George Watson accepted the cheque, seemingly impressed by the Baron's signature. Edward Green even suggested to the proprietor that he should advertise his garage as being 'by appointment to the aristocracy'!

Green drove away from West End Garage in the Daimler. Had he headed south again he might well have been able to continue his deception for a little while longer. Instead, he returned to the Atholl Palace Hotel. Unfortunately, this gave George Watson at West End Garage enough time to discover that the cheque had not been genuinely signed. It was only a short walk to the garage's bank in Atholl Street, and George Watson had wisely decided to deposit the cheque immediately. Within minutes the eagle-eyed staff at the bank recognised the cheque was fraudulent and refused to accept it. A police telegram had been sent to all bank branches warning them not to accept cheques in the name of Baron Johan Willem Quarlos Van Ufford. In the 1930s, a time when much of the banking system relied on trust, the presentation of a fraudulent cheque was considered a serious offence.

The police were informed, and a warrant was immediately issued for Edward Green's arrest.

George Watson was able to advise the police that Green had been staying at the Atholl Palace Hotel and might still be there. For a man whose quick-witted mind and plausible manner had successfully kept him one step ahead of the authorities for several weeks, Green's arrest proved a rather anticlimactic and straightforward one. He was taken away and placed on remand at Perth Prison. Friday 14th July 1933 was set as the date for his trial; to be held at Perth Sheriff's Court.

Meanwhile, the police investigation confirmed that Green was not in the employ of Baron Van Ufford; and he also appeared to have no permanent address, suggesting that he had been the perpetrator of this kind of deception for some considerable time. Edward Green appeared in court wearing an expensive smart suit, his hair immaculately swept back, and seemingly confident. Not at all the usual appearance of a prisoner who had sat on remand for several weeks. Green had clearly hoped to charm the Sheriff, in the same way that he had done to countless garage and hotel proprietors across the country.

Green's defence lawyer argued that, as he had spent a substantial amount of time on remand, he should be released with no further time served. Sheriff Valentine was in no mood for leniency, however. He recognised that Green, 'was a habitual criminal heading for a career in crime'. Citing numerous previous convictions and offences, scattered across England and Ireland, he sentenced Green to nine months imprisonment. It appeared that, using many different names, Green had made a career in the 'chauffeur' business.

So why did Edward Green use the highly conspicuous name of Baron Johan Willem Van Ufford to execute his deception? It appears that Edward Green had actually been previously employed by the Van Ufford family as a chauffeur in 1930. It was the beginning of his life in crime. Green had used his position of trust in the Van Ufford household to pilfer valuable items from under the family's nose. A confrontation followed, and he was accused of theft and dismissed by the Van Ufford's. Green saw his chauffeur scam, and the use of the Van Ufford name in his deception, as a form of sweet revenge. It might also explain how he knew enough about the movements of the Van Ufford household to enable him to present himself so convincingly. It was also assumed to be the reason he had been in possession of the blank, and presumably, stolen cheques?

The Daimler 25 was returned unharmed to the garage in London.

Upon his release Edward Green reverted to a South African name, Frank Donald Pfeff, which may, or may not, have been genuine. He even managed to find legitimate employment as a chauffeur. However, this does not seem to have kept him from returning to his old ways. He was arrested, charged, and imprisoned in 1939 with, 'obtaining food, accommodation, and services by false pretences'.

HIGHLAND PERTHSHIRE'S
UNSOLVED MYSTERIES

In the introduction to my previous book, *The River Runs Red*, I hinted at a number of unsolved and mysterious incidents from Highland Perthshire's past. Baffling events that still seem to leave more questions than answers. What really happened in these cases will, perhaps, never be known. However, one thing is certain, the events described here were never properly investigated, leaving a nagging and uneasy doubt in the mind.

During the past two centuries Perthshire newspapers often reported inexplicable tales of missing bodies, often presumed to be drowned, especially during the all-too-common bad weather that blights a Highland Perthshire winter. There was frequently an effort by loved ones to conceal any suspicion of suicide, thus avoiding any shame being brought upon their families. However, the crime statistics during the Victorian era, describe an almost lawless state existing on Highland Perthshire's roads, especially in the era prior to effective local policing. Locals walking the country roads, particularly at night, lived in constant fear of being robbed by the groups of travellers that camped in the region. Poverty, hunger, and desperation often fuelled these crimes. The authorities thought it highly likely that many people were robbed, their bodies then simply thrown into nearby rivers or lochs, with very little chance of the crime ever being solved.

The strange disappearance of a young Fearnan farmer named James Fraser is one such story. James Fraser had made the long journey by horse and cart to Aberfeldy on Tuesday 18th December 1879, apparently to transact some business at the market and the bank.

After a busy day he headed back towards Fearnan on the twisting, tree-lined Kenmore road. It was now 6pm and a cold night. After a long and weary day, James Fraser was anxious to make his way home, as soon as possible. He

had just a small lantern on his cart and perhaps may have hoped his business had been less drawn out, enabling him to have left Aberfeldy earlier. The road was already dark, with just the twinkling reflection of the moon in the river to provide an accompanying friend for the long journey. It was later speculated that he may have been carrying a large sum of money (the proceeds of goods sold at market), or that he may even have been unaware of someone following him. As darkness had already fallen, the many bends in the tree lined road would have made this a relatively easy task.

James Fraser never reached his home at Fearnan. Later in the evening, his anxious family glanced up and down the muddy roadway along the lochside at Fearnan but could see nothing. Eventually a small party left to search for him. Approximately two hours later his empty horse and cart were found wandering along the road, between Aberfeldy and Kenmore. Something sinister now seemed likely. A man would not willingly abandon his only mode of transport, as well as one of his most valuable possessions. A group of men with lanterns was hastily organised and they searched along the roadside. Finally, about a mile from Aberfeldy, James Fraser's clothes were found in a neat pile, by a bend in the road near Bolfracks, at a point where the river is closest to the road. Although his clothes lay undisturbed, there was no sign of his pocket-book, watch, or any money. The cart was also empty, although the horse seemed unharmed. Had someone taken all James Fraser's possessions from the cart? Had the horse panicked and bolted? There was no indication of that, nor any scattered debris from the cart strewn further along the roadway.

At daylight on the following morning a search of the nearby River Tay and its banks was undertaken by a large group of locals.

Had James Fraser suffered an unfortunate accident? It seems improbable. It is highly unlikely he would have stopped for a swim, or even to drink from the river on such a cold night. Had he been robbed, beaten, and thrown in the river, and his clothes then neatly arranged neatly to give the impression of suicide? It seems unlikely, however, that the perpetrator of such a despicable crime would prolong their stay at the scene and thereby risk discovery. Did James Fraser perhaps take his own life, or merely fake his death, to escape debt and discredit? This might account for his clothes being found in an ordered pile, yet there being no cash present. Certainly, this was not uncommon, and the theme was covered within the pages of *The River Runs Red* (see the cases of Rev William Bentley and of Charles Forbes). However, his family were not aware at the time of James Fraser having any money worries or pressing debt, or any that even became apparent after his death.

The untroubled state of his horse and undamaged cart also seemed to discount the likelihood of a road accident. No trace of James Fraser's body was ever found; and no further clues to his disappearance ever materialised.

During June 1891 Rev Robert Weirmouth retired to Aberfeldy for the benefit of his health. Previously at the Congregation Church at Newport in Fife, he had suffered a stroke which had affected his speech and caused a slight paralysis. He found himself no longer able to carry out the duties of his ministry; but felt sure the pleasant surroundings of Aberfeldy would aid his recovery. The Reverend spent his time enjoying regular walks in the hills surrounding the town and appeared to be in good health and improving spirits. However, on Friday 10th July he complained to his wife of a headache and resolved to go for a walk to try and shake the pain off. Rev Weirmouth set out at 6pm, heading west from Aberfeldy, along the Kenmore Road. A short distance out of Aberfeldy he turned left and followed the winding track alongside Duntuim Farm. The retired Reverend then proceeded west along the hill line, before other walkers observed him coming back down, between the Dunskaig and Duntaylor plantations. He then turned uphill again, entering the Den of Moness around 9pm. It was the height of summer and the sky still light.

Rev Wearmouth's wife became concerned around 10pm when her husband had still not returned to their home. She roused her neighbours and friends. Five search parties from among them were hastily organised and promptly began to scour the nearby hillside. However, they returned at 1am, unable to locate the missing man. More help was enlisted, and further searches were organised commencing at 2am. Unfortunately, it was now too dark to scour the hillside effectively, and so further search parties were arranged to resume at daylight on Saturday. Large gangs of searchers, including the local police, combed the tree lined and undulating hillside fruitlessly for the entire day but could find no clue to the Reverend's disappearance.

Finally, at about 6pm in the evening a telegram was received from the Post Office in Kenmore. The body of

Rev Weirmouth had been found on the south shore of Loch Tay, under the small pier in the Bay of Acharn – fully nine miles from Aberfeldy. The body was removed to Aberfeldy for examination, but no clue could be found to explain his death or disappearance. There were no marks of violence on the body, yet the Reverend's watch had stopped at quarter past four. Of course, there was no way of discerning if it had halted at 4.15 in the morning or afternoon, on either the Friday or Saturday. The authorities were completely dumbfounded. How did a man, not in the best of health, travel the nine miles from Aberfeldy? On foot, and voluntarily, the journey would take a considerable time, especially across the hill paths. Yet, there were no witnesses who could confirm seeing such a recognisable gentleman on the road, nor did any of the search parties notice him, or anyone else, along the network of footpaths. His body could not have floated there in the River Tay since the water flows rapidly in the opposite direction. No reason could be found to explain the cause of death, nor any explanation for Rev Weirmouth being found nine miles from Aberfeldy. There were no marks of violence on his body, yet his watch appeared to be broken. Not a single witness could be found, despite it being a warm evening at the height of summer, who could recall seeing him anywhere along the road from Aberfeldy to Kenmore, along the footpaths on the hillside, or at Acharn.

In Aberfeldy, on the afternoon of Tuesday 19th March 1901, the body of a local labourer was found in highly unusual circumstances. 45-year-old Alexander Brown was found, slumped forward, his head and shoulders under the surface of the water in a small burn, close to Glassie Farm, on the hillside above the town. His body was dry, with the exception of his head, which was submerged. The position of the corpse seemed odd to those who discovered it – unnatural and almost posed. There was no indication of suicide, and no one had reported any change in his recent behaviour. It was a certainly a strange position in which to attempt to take your own life. Perhaps robbery was the motive? The police could not locate his pocketbook, watch or any money, although he was thought to never go out without them. Yet there were no signs of violence or of a struggle, either on the body or the surrounding ground. Was it an accident? If so, it was a very unusual one; and surely the momentum of a sudden and accidental fall would have propelled the whole body into the water? In any case, this theory does not account for the lack of any personal possessions. Ultimately, not a single clue could be found to indicate how he met his death and the matter, it seems, will always remain a mystery.

Anybody walking along Atholl Road, in Pitlochry, in the direction of Killiecrankie will stumble upon an old, whitewashed cottage on the right-hand side at the junction with Larchwood Road. Although, in its present state, it appears to be of late eighteenth or early nineteenth-century design, it incorporates earlier structures, and is thought to be the oldest building in the town. Originally part of the Faskally Estate the building once stood alone, long before the current town developed around it.

Sunnybrae Cottage is now covered by a red painted corrugated metal roof, beneath the metal is the remnants of the cottage's last thatched roof, which was supported by two cruck frames. During the mid-18th century the cottage served as an inn, or more probably as an illegal drinking house. It appears that in 1767 John Stewart of Bonskeid and his brother-in-law Donald Stewart of Shierglas, were among a group of men drinking inside the cottage. Tempers were raised and an alcohol fuelled argument ensued. According to witnesses Donald Stewart drew his knife - he claimed it was merely to slice his food - but the gesture was interpreted as a hostile one and a large brawl broke out. John Stewart was stabbed in the chest during the melee and died from his injuries. Some doubt existed locally regarding Donald Stewart's guilt; however, he was a superstitious man and, rather than fleeing the scene, he chose to follow an old Highland folk custom and hid until his brother-in-law's funeral procession. It was said that if a murderer could see a light shining under his victim's coffin; he would escape punishment. Donald Stewart then escaped to Holland, where he remained for several years. He did eventually return home, unharmed, and was never prosecuted for the murder, which technically remains unsolved to this day.

A large, antique mantel clock from Sunnybrae Cottage now sits in the Pitlochry and Moulin Heritage Centre in the town, counting down a long-awaited vigil for justice in the case of John Stewart.

On Sunday 2nd June 1912 the body of Mr John Rae was found floating in four feet of water, at the foot of the Pass of Killiecrankie, on the River Garry. The discovery ended a month-long search for the man who had gone missing at the beginning of May.

John Rae was a well-liked and popular man from Kinloch Rannoch, where he managed a merchant's business belonging to Miss Marjory Cameron. Rae was married with three children and had just turned 47 years of age. On 1st May he had departed to Pitlochry, apparently on business, and decided to stay the night, planning to return to Kinloch Rannoch the following day. He was seen by several witnesses in Pitlochry during the day, but his movements are unaccounted for during the evening and on the following day. He would never be seen alive again. The police were never able to establish where Mr Rae had spent the night in Pitlochry, nor was he witnessed anywhere along the road northwards between Pitlochry and the spot where his body was eventually discovered. No cause could be found for his death, nor explanation for his disappearance. His widow, who identified the body, testified that he was in good spirits and could see no reason why he would take his own life.

Rumours of money difficulties at the Miss Cameron's merchants business did persist, although whether John Rae was involved is not, and probably never will be, known. What is known, however, is that all the assets of Miss Marjory Cameron were sequestered and sold, to pay off her outstanding debts, just a few months later. Had John Rae stolen money from the business, causing it to fail, and, fearing discovery, taken his own life? Had something happened in Pitlochry that caused him to suddenly change his behaviour and stay the night? Or was he confronted by person, or persons, unknown on his return journey to Kinloch Rannoch and robbed of his takings, the body then being disposed of down the steep banks of the gorge? Unfortunately, the length of time the body had spent in the water meant that any useful clues had been erased and John Rae's death remains a mystery.

In Pitlochry, on Tuesday 30th December 1930, Miss Beatrice McLarty left her family home in Faskally to take a short walk, as she did every evening. It was dark, crisp, and cold. Aged 28, dressed in a navy-blue skirt and blue coat, Beatrice said goodbye to her parents, telling them she would be back soon. She was never seen alive again.

It was concluded at the time that she may have suffered a loss of memory and accidentally wandered into the river. Yet she walked that same route almost every evening and would know of its dangers. An extensive police search of the River Tummel and the surrounding area, organised by Sergeant Cameron from Pitlochry Police Station and many employees of the Faskally Estate, searched in vain for any trace of Miss McLarty. The search continued in daylight on New Year's Eve, but their efforts proved fruitless. On New Year's Day her hat and shoes were found, a quarter of a mile away, in the Old Kennels on the estate.

Beatrice's body was eventually discovered in the river, two days later, at Dunfallandy, two miles downstream. It was presumed that she had drowned, however, the reason for her body entering the water was never resolved. There were no signs of an accident, nor had the unfortunate victim displayed any recent sign of depression or unusual behaviour. Indeed, she had enjoyed a pleasant family Christmas. Despite the time of year, the river was not especially swollen. Witnesses had reported a suspicious stranger in the area, a man seen close to the point where Beatrice's hat and shoes were found, however, he was never traced or identified. Why were her hat and shoes separate from the body? How did her body end up in the water on a dark and cold winter's evening? What had happened to her purse? Did she have a secret liaison with a lover on her regular evening walks? Despite raising these, and many other questions, the case does not appear to have been fully investigated and remains unsolved.

These mysteries offer many points of interest but sadly, no resolution. Unfortunately, they represent just a few of the many stories of unexplained disappearances in Highland Perthshire over the past 300 years. Cases which leave more questions than answers. None is stranger, however, than the case of Robert Irvine, which is documented later in this book.

THE WILD WEST FRONTIER

You may be surprised to learn that perhaps the first prototype for the typical American 'wild west' town originally existed in Perthshire.

Often referred to as the 'Dodge City' of Scotland during the 19th century, Crieff enjoyed a reputation as both a frontier town and hotbed of crime, renowned for its swift, and brutal, justice, well before the founding of its counterpart in Kansas.

A thousand years ago the Celtic chiefs chose Crieff as the administrative capital of their kingdom and an open-air court of justice was built on a Neolithic burial mound to the south of the town. This area, known as the 'Stayt', saw both justice and punishment dispensed with equal measure. The appointed representative and overseer was the Steward of Strathearn who sat on a throne-like chair and passed judgement on the cases brought before him. With full judicial omnipotence, he would frequently order the death of prisoners, who were despatched to the nearby Gallow Hill, with its infamous hanging tree.

Those lucky enough to escape the rope were likely to be punished in other ways. The town contained all the appropriate instruments of punishment and imprisonment. Stocks and jougs (hinged, iron collars chained to a wall or post) were erected in the town. When imprisonment replaced humiliation as the most popular form of punishment, a tollbooth, with cells, was added in the centre of Crieff. An iron cage was also constructed, 'large enough to contain a man and covered on the top with a lid of solid metal'. Once construction of the iron cage was completed it was firmly secured into the ground in the middle of the town, and a large hole was then excavated underneath it. This was used only for the most atrocious and desperate offenders, including those accused of witchcraft. It became known locally as 'the black hole'.

During the 15th to 18th centuries Crieff had already become an early version of the frontier towns, now associated with America's wild west. Its situation formed a natural meeting point between the Highlands of the north and the lowlands of the south. Highlanders would drive their cattle southwards, along the now forgotten cattle droves, to the great markets (or 'Trysts') at Crieff. It was not uncommon for the hillsides surrounding the town to be 'black with cattle' as tens of thousands of cattle and Highlanders, from as far away as Caithness and Orkney, gathered for the annual Michaelmas Tryst, which lasted a week. During this time the town thronged with drunken cattle drovers, bandits, cattle, and horse thieves. Tensions ran high and crime was rife. At the fair of 1723 as much as 30,000 guineas passed hands (today's equivalent of more than £1 million), as Highlanders sold their cattle to Lowlanders and English merchants. The Highlanders, having sold their cattle, then offered themselves as drovers, to escort the cattle to England, at a shilling a day!

The Highland drovers were mainly Jacobites, catholic, and vocal supporters of their cause. However, the town of Crieff at that time was largely protestant and pro-government, and (during the Trysts) was awash with Redcoats, spies and government agents. The justice delivered to criminals was swift and merciless. By the early 1700s the original hanging tree had been replaced by a formal wooden structure close to the crossing point over the River Earn, known as Gallowford Road (now more pleasantly renamed as Ford Road). The prominence of its position was no accident. Any Highlanders arriving or leaving the town would have done so along this route, taking them past the remains of bodies left hanging there to rot for months, as a warning to all would-be criminals. As they passed, the Highlanders would doff their bonnets with the words 'God bless you, and the devil damn you'.

Lord Macaulay, in his *History of England* recalls:

One day many square miles of pasture-land were swept bare by armed plunderers from the hills. Another day a score of plaids dangled in a row on the gallows of Crieff.

However, the remains of the gallows, which now reside in Perth Museum, seem to indicate that the gallows could only hold six victims at the time. Perhaps Lord Macauley wished to emphasise the strength of English justice!

The town also provided rich pickings for the cattle raiders from the north (called Caterans) who often attacked the inhabitants of the town to steal money or plunder cattle. If caught, justice was swift, and hangings became so frequent that Crieff's unenviable reputation spread across the whole of Europe. If a Highlander did manage to escape the gallows, he was often pursued through the streets of Crieff by locals and thrown in the 'drowning pool', or his ears would be sliced off as a private form of vengeance.

During the autumn of 1714 the Highlanders had gathered in Crieff for the October Tryst. These clansmen were all armed to the teeth, with pistols in their belts and broadswords hanging at their sides. During the day, fearing trouble from the famed Rob Roy and from the MacDonald clan, the town was teeming with Government spies and redcoat soldiers. One exciseman stumbled across a party from the MacDonald clan drinking untaxed whisky and, unwisely, threatened to confiscate it from them. They refused to hand the illegal liquor over and simply followed the exciseman back to his lodging. Once there, they forced their way inside, sliced off both his ears and forced him to drink the health of King James of Scotland, with the very whisky he had threatened to impound from them just minutes earlier.

However, many of the Redcoat soldiers had melted away by night-time, leaving the drunken Jacobite supporting Highlanders with a free rein over the town. Legend tells us that Rob Roy McGregor (the famed outlaw and supporter of the Jacobite cause) gathered his men in a field outside Crieff, then marched into the town square, carrying a cask of illegal whisky, and rang the town bell. As the crowd gathered, they sang songs and toasted loudly, 'His Majesty King James of Scotland!' However, one of Rob Roy's men (a wanted man) was recognised by the Redcoats, who chased him through the streets of Crieff, ultimately capturing and killing him. However, as the soldiers were distracted in their pursuit of the man, the remaining members of the McGregor clan managed to escape, vanishing into the blackness of the night.

Following the Jacobite uprising of 1715, and defeat at the Battle of Sheriffmuir, 350 returning Highlanders ransacked Crieff and Muthill on the bitterly cold night of 26th January 1716. The Highlanders torched the towns in a bloody revenge - partly as a reprisal for the town's support of the government forces, and partly as a 'scorched earth' policy. It was later reported that:

On that night every dwelling house in the town was burned to the ground, and, men, women, and children were left exposed in the open fields, with scarcely a rag to cover them from the extreme severity of the season.

The Jacobite rebels started at the west end of the town, burning the house of Thomas Caw. They then moved to the neighbouring house, which belonged to Caw's eighty-year-old father. As Caw tried to save his father, he pleaded with the Highlanders: 'For God's sake, allow me to take out my father that he not perish in the flames!' The rebels replied, 'Let them all burn together!'

The houses of the rich were ransacked first, and eighteen horses were stolen, to help with the removal of the Jacobites' ill-gotten gains. Those who resisted were severely beaten. Had the Jacobites not been acutely aware of the presence of Colonel Campbell's Government troops close by the atrocities may have been worse, with many more losing their lives.

Most of Crieff was destroyed during the course of the night. The town that we see today is a very different one, and was laid out by James Drummond, the 3rd Duke of Perth, from 1731 onwards, mainly as part of the establishment of the town's textile industry.

Such were the high numbers of executions in Crieff that the town actually employed its own full-time hangman until 1746, one of the only places in Britain to do so. The position was a busy one, with the hangman well paid, and his services were regularly requested by other towns and cities. Donald McCarie eventually became the final hangman in Crieff. His prestigious position brought with it a property, the Hangman's House, a supply of meal, and a salary of £27 9s (approximately £7,000 today).

Following the abolition of hereditary jurisdiction in 1748, however, Crieff's reputation as a place of severe punishment receded.

Perhaps the most infamous, and also the last, execution in Crieff (of which evidence still exists), occurred in June 1681. The Bishop of Dunkeld received a complaint against Richard Duncan, the 35-year-old minister of Kinkell Parish, near Crieff. Duncan was accused of 'scandalous offences' and a decree was issued by the bishop:

A visitation shall be held at the Kirk of Trinity Park for the tryal of any scandal laid to the charge of Mr Richard Duncan, minister there.

Following the investigation, Richard Duncan was deposed from office and removed from his residence, the Manse. The church then undertook some alterations to the Manse and, to the horror of the workmen, the body of a child was found, buried underneath the hearthstone. It was alleged that Duncan had fathered a child, born by his maid servant, and had either killed the child, or somehow been complicit in its death. A hasty trial was held, presided over by James Drummond, the Earl of Perth. The Drummond family wielded enormous power and influence in Crieff (including the right to levy monies on all cattle sold at the annual Trysts). The decision was a foregone conclusion and Richard Duncan was sentenced to be hung at Crieff gallows.

However, the Earl of Perth's son (also called James) and many local parishioners were not so convinced of Duncan's guilt. Duncan, himself, had always professed his innocence. Considerable effort was put into obtaining a reprieve for the erstwhile minister, including from Lord Fountainhall (one of Scotland's foremost legal experts) who proclaimed that, 'he has been convicted on very slender presumptions.'

Eventually, a pardon was secured on the very day of Richard Duncan's execution. A messenger, carrying the reprieve, was despatched to 'ride like the wind' to Crieff but had only reached Muthill (just three miles away) by the allotted hour. Meanwhile, Richard Duncan was led to the scaffold where he once again loudly declared his innocence. Duncan told those present that his lack of guilt would be proved by the presence of a white dove, which would land on the scaffold, at the exact moment of his passing. Local legend tells us that this actually happened.

The messenger, bearing the pardon, arrived just minutes too late. A verse, written in the old Scots dialect, marks the incident:

Oh, what a parish, a terrible parish
Oh, what a parish is that o' Kinkell;
They hangit their minister, droon'd their precentor*,
Dang doon** the steeple and fuddled the bell.

*A precentor was responsible for leading the congregation in the singing of hymns, prior to the presence of organs in churches. This line also refers to a previous incident in which the precentor of the church had drowned in suspicious circumstances while crossing the river.

** Dang doon – pulled down

Bonnie Prince Charlie stayed in Crieff, on his way to Culloden in April 1746. However, the heavy defeat suffered by the Jacobites at the battle saw stringent and punitive measures enforced by the Crown over those wishing to continue the Highland way of life. The wearing of tartan, singing of traditional songs and the playing of bagpipes was banned. The Gaelic language (already banned in 1616 by the Crown) was supressed even further. Even the rich and influential Drummond family did not escape the English backlash after Culloden. The Reverend Robert Lyon Drummond, who had welcomed Bonnie Prince Charlie to Crieff just days earlier, was imprisoned in Carlisle as a Jacobite sympathiser and executed along with 75 others.

Crieff was later mentioned in a remarkable article called *The Sheep Stealer*, written under the pseudonym The Wayfarer, in which the town is given credit for its part in civilising the Highlanders and suppressing their Jacobite tendencies:

I am inclined to think that the muse of history has not given Crieff the credit to which it is entitled for its efforts to civilise the Highlander. The town did more in this direction than any other, and today when you visit it on business or pleasure the natives point out to you with some pride the gallows tree upon which half a dozen red and black haired Highlanders in kilts, sporrans, and sgain dubh *(small single-edged knife), dangled, not for a day, to make sure the breath had left them, but for months until the birds of the air had picked their bones and made nests of their hair.*

Over time, the large groups of Highlanders congregating in the town gradually lessened, and the need for a full-time hangman was deemed no longer necessary. By 1770 the cattle tryst was removed to Falkirk Muir and many of the drovers now bypassed Crieff altogether.

Eventually the gallows were dismantled and Crieff became more associated with the textile industry and, later, as a Victorian health resort, with the opening of the Hydro Hotel.

Yet its reputation stands at odds with the name given to the gallows in the town. They were known throughout the country, and beyond, as the 'Kind Gallows of Crieff.'

'Kind', apparently because they had been constructed with an abnormally long drop for the victim. This meant death would result far more quickly and with less suffering than might usually be expected.

THE ABERFELDY RIOTS

Riots in the street are usually associated with long, warm summer evenings when the streets are busy and the hot nights cause tempers to fray. That, however, was not the case in Aberfeldy on the evening of Saturday 28th November 1903. In fact, the weather had been extraordinarily wet that autumn - he previous seven weeks having seen more rain than at any time in the last 50 years.

Despite the dark night and the wintry chill, a sizeable throng of young men had gathered in the newly completed Square and along both Chapel Street and Bank Street. Chapel Street at the time was notorious for its drunken and unruly inhabitants. Many of the impoverished residents of the street often found themselves on the wrong side of the law, normally for petty offences of drunkenness or domestic confrontation. However, the events of Saturday 28th November were far beyond that which was usually associated with the worst excesses of the town.

Under the gas street lighting the large, and unruly, group were, according to locals, 'openly drinking in the street, parading, shouting, and causing a good deal of disturbance'. Glasses were smashed as the group's behaviour worsened. Those not wishing to be caught up in the fracas hurried home. Residents locked their doors and the local police constables vainly attempted to restore order. Aberfeldy had not seen conduct of this nature for many years and the constables were jeered and booed by the crowd as tempers frayed to breaking point.

A perceptible undercurrent of tension had been noticeable in Aberfeldy during the autumn of 1903; and had been remarked upon by many in the town. The recent opening of Victoria Park by Lady Breadalbane had seemingly highlighted class hostilities in the town. The ostentatious display of wealth exhibited in the celebrations served to emphasis the growing chasm in Aberfeldy between the rich landowners, the wealthy influx of new merchants, and the poorer working classes forced to live in rundown accommodation.

Tensions in the Cape Colonies had seen young men from Aberfeldy sent thousands of miles from home to fight the

Boers. There had been several recent arrests in the town for drunkenness, usually among young men letting off some steam. Many, among the working class in the town, had felt these arrests unjust. And the growing movement in favour of universal suffrage for women, which seemed to some to be yet another threat to long held tradition, had been exacerbated by the recent launch of the *Daily Mirror* – 'a paper for women, run by women.'

On the night of 28th November, the police constables kept a close eye, looking for potential troublemakers. John McInnes, a local man and well-known to the Perthshire police, seemed to be the leader of the group and was singled out and warned by the officers, as they endeavoured to disperse the crowd surrounding him. Despite several warnings the drunken McInnes refused to move and became openly aggressive and abusive. Fearing an escalation in violence, the constables stepped in and arrested McInnes in front of the jeering mob. It was a brave, if foolhardy, decision as the officers were hopelessly outnumbered.

Sergeant Campbell and one of his constables apprehended McInnes and insisted that he accompany them along the street to the police station. McInnes refused, swearing and yelling abuse at the officers. His bravado seemed to spread to the crowd of fifty or so men, who joined in, shouting, and throwing glasses, stones, and any objects they could lay their hands on. Fearing that McInnes would escape from their grasp, the police were left with little alternative but to drag their prisoner unceremoniously along the road, his heels scraping along the ground, as he resisted furiously.

Struggling, screaming, and kicking violently, McInnes shouted to the following mob to assist him. Clearly fearing for their own safety, the police bravely continued to drag McInnes along the street until they reached the door of Aberfeldy Police Station. However, as they attempted to pull him inside, and behind the safety of the sturdy door, the mob descended on them. Jostled and kicked to the ground, the small handful of officers were hopelessly outnumbered. They lost control of McInnes, who quickly got to his feet and returned to the centre of the group. Cheers erupted from the mob who, treating McInnes like a returning war hero, carried him shoulder high back down the street towards the Square.

A section of the throng remained outside the police station, hellbent on revenge for the treatment of their friend, and hurled objects against doors and windows and surrounded the police station, leaving the men inside with no means of escape. Thinking quickly, the officers barricaded themselves inside the building, moving furniture against the door and piling bookcases and cabinets in front of the windows. However, still inflamed by the perceived injustice towards John McInnes, the group made one last attempt to force their way inside the station. Led by another well-known troublemaker, James Laird, the throng were unsuccessful in their efforts; fortunately for the safety of the constables trapped inside, the door stood firm.

Realising that their point had been made, and with little else left to prove, tempers seemed to calm slightly and the mob gradually dispersed, leaving the police officers to lick their wounds. They wisely remained inside the police station until daylight arrived and brought with it a degree of safety. The streets now seemed quiet, with just the debris from the previous evening left as a reminder of the troubles.

McInnes, as mentioned earlier, was already known to the authorities and it would prove to be a simple task to locate him on the following day. He was re-arrested on the Sunday morning as he attempted to sleep off his hangover and, according to witnesses, protested his innocence as he was unceremoniously led away; claiming to the officers, 'You have the wrong man' and 'I am supposed to be going to church.'

He was taken to Perth Police Station in a special cell-wagon, brought to Aberfeldy especially for the purpose. The wagon was parked in the Square for maximum effect and to clearly send a message to any of the previous night's mob who may have considered reigniting the previous night's embers of resentment. This time a dozen or so police constables attended, standing menacingly in line, with their life preservers (truncheons) at the ready, determined to ensure there would be no repeat of the behaviour encountered on the previous evening.

James Laird, the other ringleader from Saturday night's disturbances, was also arrested, and the pair appeared before Sheriff Sym at Perth Sheriff's Court on the Monday morning. Laird was described in court as a 'drunken character who has passed through the hands of the police before' (he had a previous conviction for assault).

However, there was to be no repeat of the pair's bravado

during their drunken antics from Saturday evening. This time, as they stood shamefaced in front of Sheriff Sym, McInnes and Laird's demeanour was far more contrite. Both men appeared very much the worse for wear. They looked down at the floor of the courtroom, shuffling from side to side as they did so, holding their caps in their hands, and generally appeared to be thoroughly ashamed. The *Perthshire Advertiser*, clearly appalled by the scenes of the preceding evening in Aberfeldy, had despatched a reporter to the court. He described the riot as 'extraordinary and unparalleled in Aberfeldy's history'. Both men, it was reported, were 'exceedingly penitent and downcast' as they prepared to face the wrath of Sheriff Sym.

John McInnes was charged as follows:

Having on Saturday last in Bank Street and Chapel Street, Aberfeldy, cursed and swore, behaved in a disorderly manner, and committed a breach of the peace, and then resisting arrest by the police constables, in a violent manner.

However, despite their remorseful outward appearance, it seems that a night in the police cells had not changed either man's attitude to authority. McInnes entered a not guilty plea, claiming he was not responsible for his actions 'after taking on board some spirits or beer.'

James Laird was then charged as follows:

Having, in Chapel Street, Aberfeldy, on Saturday last, having assaulted Police Sergeant Campbell and a police constable while on duty, by pushing and jostling them about, tripping them, and injuring them by kicking them, and attempting to get out of their custody the previous prisoner.

Laird also entered a not guilty plea, stating to the court that he was not responsible for his actions, 'when under the influence of the drink'.

Prosecuting, Mr Melville Jameson informed the court that, following the arrest of McInnes, Laird clearly became the ringleader of the group and had not only led the mob to the police station but had incited the crowd to rescue McInnes from his incarceration.

Sheriff Sym was in no mood to accept the excuse of 'the drink' being to blame, which both men claimed was the reason for their unruly behaviour. Neither was the Sheriff impressed by their attempt to blame the rough treatment they had received from the police as a mitigating factor in their actions. In fact, the police constables were praised for both their actions and their bravery.

Sheriff Sym stated, in response to the men's defence:

I am not disposed to do anything to make it difficult for the police of Aberfeldy to do their duty. John McInnes, you will be fined 40 shillings (approximately £250 today), *with the alternative of 14 days' imprisonment, while James Laird, you will be sent to prison for 15 days.*

McInnes could not afford to pay the fine and chose to spend his sentence in Perth Prison. Suitably admonished and much the worse for wear, the pair eventually returned to Aberfeldy two weeks later. Although their return was greeted with cheers by their comrades, there does not seem to have been a repeat of the events of Saturday 28th

November 1903. The police also wisely kept an increased presence in the town for several weeks following McInnes and Laird's release.

The riot had been the worst incident in living memory in the usually quiet town. Aberfeldy had not seen such disturbances since the election of the Liberal MP Sir Donald Currie to Parliament, during the General Election of spring 1880, when drunken rioters had paraded around the streets, smashing the windows of prominent local Tories. As the behaviour of rioters worsened on that night, Sir Robert Menzies, the local Tory candidate, wisely fled across Wades Bridge to the safety of his family home, Castle Menzies in Weem!

ASSAULT WITH
A CUT-THROAT RAZOR

It was 13th April 1914. George Bernard Shaw's *Pygmalion* had just opened in London and, as the fight for women's suffrage continued, the Suffragettes were in the middle of a campaign of arson attacks throughout the country, including the firebombing of post-boxes in Perth. War in Europe was still four months away as Scotland enjoyed some unseasonably pleasant early spring weather.

In the bustling centre of Perth, Mrs Jessie Campbell, a petite middle-aged woman, went about her daily business as usual. Her life was an unhappy one with little joy. Ten years previously she had argued with her husband, James, and he had subsequently moved out of the two rooms the couple had shared at 13 Cow Vennel, a narrow and dimly lit city centre passageway, lined with doors leading to lodgings, and drying-yards filled with damp laundry. The dark and dingy thoroughfare, between South Street and Canal Street, was cramped and the accommodation even more so.

Jessie Campbell's dreary dwelling consisted of just two rooms, a kitchen/living room facing the Vennel and a bedroom, with a small window which overlooked the enclosed yard at the back. Mrs Campbell and her estranged husband had a grown-up daughter, Mary Ann, aged 21, who was employed at Messrs Coates Bros Ltd, the spinning mill in Balhousie. Mary Ann sometimes stayed with her mother at 13 Cow Vennel, and sometimes at her father's new lodgings in New Row. Occasionally her father would return to No. 13 to visit Mary Ann and her mother, but it was usually short-lived, and he would leave again suddenly.

During her father's long absences Mary Ann's mother, Jessie, had taken up with another man. William Mitchell was an imposing, sullen, intimidating, and hot-tempered man. At 57, he was older than Mrs Campbell and drank heavily. His mood invariably became progressively worse under the influence of drink. Young Mary Ann found the atmosphere more and more uncomfortable when Mitchell, a blacksmith by trade, was present in her mother's house. She often noticed his lurid glances, followed by suggestive remarks, which made her more and more uncomfortable. Mary Ann was an attractive and slim girl, and despite her limited funds she dressed to the fashion of the era in hourglass corsets, long narrow skirts, and ankle boots.

After he had consumed a bottle or two of beer Mitchell would frequently put his arm around Mary Ann's narrow waist and ask her to sit on his lap. He would often invent excuses to send Mrs Campbell out on an errand, usually on the pretext of fetching drink or tobacco for him, so he could be alone with Mary Ann in the claustrophobic two room apartment. Mitchell would then attempt to seduce her; telling her that he could teach her everything she needed to know to be a real woman; but Mary Ann resisted his advances time and time again. Neighbours often reported hearing shouting and screaming echoing in the Cow Vennel, as Mitchell lost his temper at Mary Ann's indifference to him.

Not wanting to upset her mother, by telling her the truth, Mary Ann decided to move in permanently with her father in New Row, and only to visit her mother again if she knew Mitchell was not at home. This incensed William Mitchell even further and he angrily followed Mary Ann to her father's house, demanding to be let in. Mary Ann and her father refused to admit him. Mitchell would return again and again – usually in a state of drunkenness - until finally Mr Campbell forcibly ejected him from the premises, with the help of the Perth City Police. Mitchell returned skulking to the dimly lit lodgings at No 13 muttering how he intended to take his revenge for being spurned. The same chain of events continued for many weeks. On each occasion Mitchell was left, fuming with rage, his temper raised, and his ardour inflamed. He was, as the newspapers would later report, 'determined to force his unwanted attentions on Mary in this sordid little affair'.

On the evening of 13th April 1914, Mary Ann had finished a hard day's work at the Balhousie Mill in Perth and believing Mitchell not to be at home, decided to call on her mother in the Cow Vennel. Once there, Mary Ann offered to assist her mother by taking some clothes and linen away to be washed at the public washrooms and laundry.

The laundry took Mary Ann two hours, and when she at last returned to No. 13 Cow Vennel the lamplighters were busy lighting the flickering gaslights in the streets. It was past 7 o'clock and she was exhausted. Her mother gratefully offered to make Mary a cup of tea, bringing some water to boil on the stove. Suddenly, to Mary Ann's surprise William Mitchell appeared in the doorway, which led from the bedroom into the kitchen. She had been unaware that he was in the house. Mary was naturally nervous, however, Mitchell appeared to be relaxed and less volatile than of late. She also felt slightly more comfortable with her mother present; and did not want to leave having only just returned from carrying the large basket of heavy washing. The three sat down around the small table and drank their tea, chatting. The mood seemed to be a little lighter. Mitchell suggested that they all share a bottle of beer. He gave Jessie Campbell three halfpennies and ordered her to go and purchase three bottles of beer in South Street. Dutifully she left, leaving her daughter alone with Mitchell.

Within seconds of the door closing, Mitchell's demeanour changed. His face darkened as he slowly stood up, rolling up his sleeves. Approaching Mary Ann, who was cornered in the small room, he produced a cut-throat razor from the pocket of his grubby waistcoat, saying to the terrified

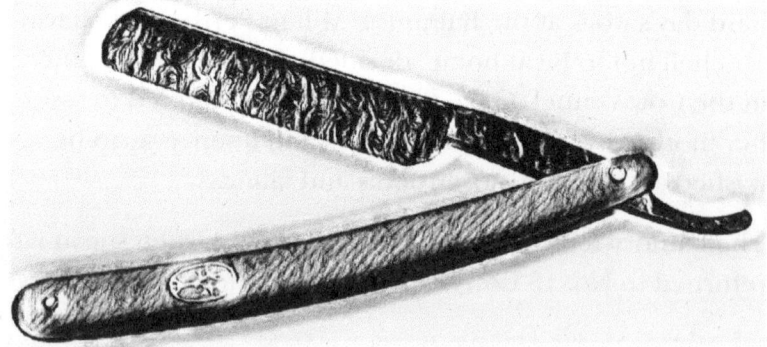

girl, 'Mary, you are about to undergo the experience of a lifetime!', as he menacingly unsheathed the sharp steel blade. Mary Ann screamed but the noise was drowned out by the sound of children playing outside and the general hubbub from the busy streets surrounding the narrow alleyway. Mitchell grabbed Mary Ann's forearm with his left hand, as she resisted with all her strength. His face like thunder at her rejection of him, Mitchell swung the razor savagely towards her, slashing left and right, in a murderous onslaught. Mary Ann attempted to defend herself. She automatically raised her arms, partly in terror, and partly in an instinctive reaction of self-preservation. Mitchell slashed her forearms and neck, cutting her deeply in five places. Blood spurted from the wounds onto the stone floor and covered Mary Ann's shoulders, face, and arms. In that moment, as Mary Ann grasped the desperation of her situation, a sudden steeliness came over her.

In a split second her only course of action became clear. Instead of pulling backwards and away from Mitchell, as might be expected, she lunged towards him, momentarily taking him by surprise. He was knocked backwards, colliding with the kitchen table; and jolted off balance just long enough for Mary Ann to make her escape through the kitchen door and into the passageway outside. She left a vivid trail of blood on the floor of the kitchen, along the Cow Vennel and past a group of children playing outside. Her blouse and skirt were now stained red with the gushing blood. Screaming 'Murder! Murder!', she knocked frantically on the door of the nearest neighbour, Mrs Angus. Mary Ann shouted for help and, desperately holding her hands tightly over the serious wound on her neck, pleaded for water. Mrs Angus, perhaps in shock or perhaps in fear, replied 'For God's sake Mary, get out, I cannot stand the sight of blood!'

Mary Ann, dazed and about to faint, turned and staggered the few yards from the narrow alleyway onto the wide and busy South Street, her outfit now drenched in blood and her wounds bleeding copiously. Still frightened for her life and now falling into a blurry state of unconsciousness, she briefly glanced back, but Mitchell did not seem to be behind her.

The sight of the bleeding and obviously distressed young woman caused a panic among the passers-by. Luckily for Mary Ann, the local police surgeon Dr Parker-Stewart was taking his usual evening stroll along South Street. He attempted to staunch the flow of blood and persuaded several others to assist him in carrying her back to the house of Mrs Angus in the Cow Vennel. Once inside they carefully laid Mary Ann on the kitchen table and the doctor attempted to dress the wounds with whatever fabrics he could lay to hand. Meanwhile, the police were sent for, and a cab was hailed to race Mary Ann to the Royal Infirmary as quickly as possible.

The police arrived quickly and officers, armed with lanterns and truncheons, entered through the kitchen door into 13 Cow Vennel. The kitchen was empty, apart from the still-lit stove, the evidence of the struggle, and the bloodstained floor. Realising that the back room had a window onto the yard, officers guessed that Mitchell had made his escape across the yard, and perhaps evaded capture through one of the other properties adjoining the yard.

However, on entering the back room, the constables made a shocking discovery. Mitchell was slumped to his knees on the floor, next to a single wooden chair in the corner of the dimly lit room. His chin was resting on his chest, his left hand resting on the chair and his right hand still firmly clasping the opened razor. Both his body and the floor were covered in pools of blood and, as the policemen's eyes became accustomed to the gloom, they realised Mitchell had cut his own throat from ear to ear. The cut was so savage and so deep he had nearly severed his own head from his neck. Bone and tissue were clearly visible to the horrified constables as they reeled backwards in horror. So deep was the wound that the rapid exsanguination had already given Mitchell's features a ghostlike appearance, the like of which the police officers had never seen before. He had clearly died within a matter of seconds. The look of horror and anguish on Mitchell's twisted face haunted those in attendance for many months afterwards.

Meanwhile, Mary Ann was rushed to Perth Royal Infirmary and operated on immediately. In acute pain, she was placed under chloroform for 90 minutes while doctors attempted to staunch the bleeding and stitch her wounds. Mary Ann had sustained five deep and traumatic injuries, four to the arms and one to the side of her neck. Besides the deeper wounds, her arms and hands were severely lacerated with at least fifteen minor wounds; and she had also lost a great deal of blood. Doctors managed to halt the flow, but the heavy loss of blood and the risk of septic poisoning and infection (in the days before antibiotics), meant that she was not expected to live. The *Perthshire Advertiser*, the main source of news for the people of Perth in the days before television and radio, informed the public that Mary Ann would likely not survive.

Her condition did not improve for several days, and the press reported that her lack of progress was extremely worrying. The public rushed to buy the latest edition in the hope of updated news. Mary Ann's case caused a sensation in Perth, and gripped the population, who waited on tenterhooks for an outcome to the story. Neighbours called on Mary Ann's mother, the distraught and hysterical Jessie Campbell, who had returned to her lodging in Cow Vennel on the night of the attack to discover pools of blood, police officers, and utter mayhem. Her neighbours comforted her, as best they could, and helped scrub the blood from the stone floor.

Cut-throat razors were widely used and available in 1914 and were a common weapon in cases of domestic assault and suicide. With the invention of the safety razor cut-throat razors largely disappeared from public sale, becoming the preserve of barbers.

Happily, Mary Ann did make an eventual and a slow recovery, the *Perthshire Advertiser* reporting a few weeks later that 'she is now progressing satisfactorily, however her escape from death was by the narrowest of margins.' She bore the marks of the attack for the rest of her life. She eventually married in 1922 and remained in Perth for the remainder of her life.

William Mitchell's cause of death was reported by the coroner as 'extreme exsanguination resulting in instant death'. He also remarked on 'the evil wickedness and cowardice of a man who could both attack a young girl and seek to escape justice'. Many at the hearing sat in disbelief as the extent of Mitchell's wounds were revealed, perhaps wondering in what state of mind a human being must be to inflict such violence and pain on themselves and others.

WHERE IS ARTHUR IRVINE?

The population of Highland Perthshire woke on New Year's Day 1913 to be greeted by sunshine and the prospect of a bright, clear, and crisp day. Reports of the discovery of Captain Scott's body in the Antarctic were just reaching Britain, Arthur Conan Doyle had just published *The Lost World*, and the forerunner of Lucozade – Glucozade – appeared on the shelves of Scottish shops for the first time.

Many people slept on that morning, nursing sore heads from the previous evening's celebrations; however, Arthur Irvine was awake, dressed, and full of energy, bright and early. He first planned to visit his elderly mother, Ann, in Ballinluig, then catch the 10.30am train from Ballinluig Halt to Perth, reaching the city in time to watch St Johnstone play Abercorn in the New Year's Day fixture. He buttoned up his dark overcoat, lifted his collar to the wind, put his cap on and left his cottage at Tomnafennag, Pitcastle, near Strathtay, telling friends and family he would return by a later train. He took the train from Grandtully Station, along with a handful of other passengers, as it snaked alongside the river, clattering over the bridge at Logierait, finally pulling into Ballinluig Halt. Arthur Irvine briskly walked across the fields to his mother's home, keeping an eye on the time. After he had wished his mother a 'happy new year', promising to call again the following day, he returned to the station platform in time to catch the 10.30 train to Perth.

Arthur Bentwick Irvine was likeable, and a popular man locally. Aged 52, he was a mason employed by Atholl Estates and a member of the local curling club. He chatted to fellow passengers as the train chuntered along the tree lined route into Perth. On arriving at Perth General railway station, he alighted and joined a large group of other supporters on the short walk along King's Place, in the winter sunshine, to the Recreation Grounds (near to the current South Inch) to watch the football match. During the course of the game, he was witnessed by several spectators, who were later confidently able to confirm to the Perth police that Irvine was definitely a spectator at the ground; some even remembered talking to him.

Following the 1-1 draw between the two sides, he joined the many supporters who made their way along Princes Street onto Canal Street and South Street to share a drink at one of the many public houses in the centre of Perth. Irvine was again seen by several witnesses enjoying a beer and chatting with other supporters, immediately after the match, and later on South Street and, some thought, on High Street too. No one could remember or confirm the last known sighting of Arthur Irvine, but he was not seen returning to Pitlochry by any of the trains later that evening. Not a single passenger on any of the evening trains, ticket collector, platform ticket holder, nor any employee of the railway company at any of the stations, could remember seeing him either.

By the following morning, Thursday 2nd January, his family were distraught with worry. Arthur Irvine usually spent significant periods of time at home with his family. He was not a heavy drinker, did not go out a great deal, and it was very unusual for him to be absent from home for more than a few hours at a time. He visited his aged mother nearly every day and he had promised to call on her again that morning. His brother, Peter, who was also a mason for the Atholl Estate, contacted the local police and offered to co-ordinate a search from his home at Moulinearn in Ballinluig. Peter, together with the police, issued a description to the *Perthshire Advertiser* and the *Dundee Courier*, in the hope that someone would recognise Arthur's description and report his whereabouts:

Mr Arthur Irvine is 52 years of age, 5 feet 8 or 9 inches in height, ordinary build, fresh complexion, rather thin features, fairish hair, grey at temples, with brown moustache, but otherwise clean shaven. When he left for Perth on the first day of the year he was dressed in black serge trousers, greenish mixture coat and vest, with dark overcoat, grey cap, and collar and tie above a primary shirt. The missing man, who is a native of Ballinluig, had an abscess mark on the right cheek and also on the left jaw. He had in his possession a black pocket-watch.

This description was widely distributed during that first week in January and, when this provided no positive results, it was circulated again during the second week of the month. Although hampered by bad weather and limited hours of daylight, police searched along the railway line between Perth and Ballinluig; but could find no clue as to Arthur Irvine's whereabouts. There had been no sightings of Arthur in the meantime, either in Perth or anywhere else. The plea for information placed in the local newspapers also received no response. Two weeks later, impatient and fraught with worry, his bother Peter Irvine was about to organise a local meeting, in the hope of raising volunteers for an extended search, when he received a telegram from Perth police - could he proceed to Perth Mortuary as soon as possible, where his help would be needed to identify a body that had been recovered from the River Tay in Perth?

On the morning of Wednesday 15th January, two Perth labourers, James Colgan and James Gardiner, had been walking from their lodging in Meal Vennel alongside the River Tay, close to the Gasworks. The men observed what looked like a body floating in the dark water about 15 feet from the south bank. A local police constable was summoned and, together, the three men waded into the water and brought the body to the shoreline. The local undertakers removed the corpse to the mortuary and the newspapers were informed that the body of Arthur Irvine had been located.

Peter Irvine arrived at Perth Mortuary on the same afternoon and was shown the body by the coroner. However, much to Peter's relief the body, although similar in age and build, was not that of his brother Arthur. The coroner and the police were astounded. So certain were they that the body must be that of Arthur Irvine, that a full examination was yet to take place. The similarities were certainly uncanny. A full description of the newly discovered, and as yet unknown, victim was also issued to the press:

The body is that of a man from 45 to 50 years of age, 5 feet 6 or 7 inches in height, fair brown hair and moustache slightly mixed with grey – otherwise cleanshaven. He was dressed in a dark blue serge suit.

Strangely, the mysterious unidentified body was dressed in four shirts, all worn over the top of each other. On the inside collar of the second shirt was the figure '3', and below it the letter 'B', and below that 'Hyam, Edinburgh, Dublin and Belfast'. Inside the victim's jacket pocket was a purse containing half a sovereign, two half crowns and one shilling. A further examination of the trouser pockets revealed a third-class railway return for New Year's Day, the same day that Arthur Irvine had gone missing – from Invergordon to Glasgow Buchanan Street, and a blank counterfoil for a 6-shilling postal order. It was estimated that the body had been in the water for at least a week, more probably two.

The Perth police now had two missing men, both similar in appearance, both having taken railway journeys, and both apparently seeming to have disappeared on the same day. Crucially, however, they only had one body. There was still no sign of Arthur Irvine.

Heavy snowfall had meanwhile hindered any meaningful examination of the land adjoining the railway line between Perth and Ballinluig; and ice had made searching the lochs and rivers equally challenging too. Especially as the lochs had not been frozen on the day that Arthur Irvine had gone missing. The decision was made to issue two further requests to the newspapers, one pleading for help to identify the mysterious body fished from the River Tay, and a second to appeal for more clues in the search for Arthur Irvine. It was now 18 full days since his disappearance.

Meanwhile in Ballinluig, the local community, already distraught over the disappearance of the popular Arthur Irvine, were also enduring yet another missing person case. A young mother, named Annie Gordon, had vanished from the area, taking her eleven-year-old daughter with her. After an absence of four weeks the mother and daughter were spotted on the banks of the River Almond, near Perth. Annie Gordon had bound herself and her daughter together and attempted to roll down the bank in an attempt to end both their lives. Fortunately, the endeavour had failed, and the shock of hitting the cold water seemed to bring Annie Gordon to her senses. She handed herself and her daughter in to the local police station, tired, cold, and hungry. They had not eaten for three days. Annie Gordon was removed to Perth District Lunatic Asylum at Murthly, and her daughter was sent to live with relatives. The community of Ballinluig hoped that they would not have to endure another tragedy or scandal within the same week.

Two days later, on 20th January, the police at last made further breakthroughs in both cases. The Watson family from Whyte Street in Govan, Glasgow, recognised the description of the man found in the water, as that of their brother Robert, aged 53. He had been employed as a shipwright in the Glasgow Docks. Robert Watson had been away for New Year visiting his parents in Cromarty and had last been seen on 6th January. No clue was ever found to explain how his body had ended up in the River Tay, 133 miles from his parent's house in Cromarty and 67 miles away from his own home in Govan. Nor was any cause of death ever determined.

Prompted by the fresh newspaper appeal in the search for Arthur Irvine, a further witness came forward. He was able to confirm to police that he had definitely seen Irvine on Perth High Street at a much later time on New Year's Day than any of the other previous witnesses could testify to. However, this simply raised more questions since his movements on the afternoon in question seem to have been away from, rather than towards, the railway station.

A further ten days passed before the snow had finally melted enough for another organised search to begin. A request was placed in the *Dundee Courier* newspaper on

Thursday 30th January appealing for volunteers to help mount an extensive search of all road and railway verges between Ballinluig and Perth. Mr William MacIntosh, a former friend of Arthur Irvine's organised the parties. Although it was now a month since Irvine's disappearance, not a single clue or sighting had yet come to light.

On Saturday February 8th, 125 men - at that time, the largest official search party ever organised in Perthshire - began an extensive search of woodlands, verges, and roadsides between Perth and Pitlochry. The largest group started from Pitlochry and headed south towards Perth, painstakingly searching all the roadside verges, ditches and side roads on the way. Another section searched from Dunkeld Railway Station, in a southward direction along the railway embankments. The final group began at Dunkeld and worked their way northwards. Unfortunately, all their efforts proved fruitless. The following morning, yet another large party met at Ballinluig and began a comprehensive search of all woodland in and around the village. As on the previous day, however, their efforts went unrewarded and they trudged home weary, cold, and disconsolate.

Finally, the news that his family were dreading came on Thursday March 13th – just four days before what would have been Arthur Irvine's 53rd birthday. A body, in an advanced state of decomposition, was found floating among the reeds on the left bank of the River Tay, close to Hill Farm at Errol, several miles downstream from Perth city centre. Any hope of determining a cause of death was rendered impossible due to the decay and damage caused by the prolonged exposure to water. The County Police at Errol, and Irvine's six brothers and sisters were forced to make an identification based on the clothing and the personal possessions found on the victim, although even this proved difficult, as the body seemed to be devoid of anything that might prove useful.

Had Arthur Irvine suffered a tragic accident, or was he the victim of something more sinister? His money and watch were never recovered, either from his body, anywhere in Perth, or along the river. Despite an extensive search of the river in Perth it had taken more than two months to locate Arthur's body. Had he been in the river all that time? Many thought it unlikely, although his corpse was in an advanced state of decomposition.

Was he the victim of a violent attack? That seemed to be the most likely scenario, which would account for his missing money and watch. A man might lose his wallet, but to lose a watch seems less likely. Did he suffer a tragic accident? This was a possible solution to his mysterious death; however, it is difficult to accidently fall into a river and Irvine was not a heavy drinker. Suicide also seemed highly improbable, as Irvine was well-liked, had no money troubles and had promised to visit his mother the following day. Suicide also did not explain his missing money and watch.

How his body had ended up in the River Tay, in the opposite direction from his supposed journey from Perth city centre towards his intended destination at Ballinluig, will probably always remain a mystery.

THE BLAIRGOWRIE MYSTERY

The year 1730 was a remarkable one for the town of Blairgowrie in Perthshire. An uneasy fear and commotion had enveloped the whole parish, caused by the extraordinary revelations of William Soutar, a tenant of Middle Mause, at the Mains of Mause close to the town. William Soutar declared, to a shocked group of locals, that he had been ordered by a supernatural being, 'to search for human bones secretly buried in a place known as The Isle.'

Soutar also claimed that he had been:

Informed by the ghostly presence that the burial site was situated between two or three small streams on the estate of Roehalzie, near the south-east march, adjacent to the old turnpike road from Blairgowrie to Bridge of Cally, which passes up by Woodhead.

The apparition that appeared to William Soutar, did so in the form of a large dog, yet spoke with a human voice. The animal declared itself to be the reincarnation of David Soutar, a man who had fled the country, after having killed a man at 'The Isle' 35 years earlier. The supernatural animal instructed William Soutar that the bones must now be disinterred and receive a proper burial in a churchyard. The spectre of David Soutar explained that he had been forced to take the bestial form, for all eternity, because his dog had also been instrumental in the murder.

William Soutar's description of the events was given much credence in Blairgowrie as the story of a man disappearing in mysterious circumstances, in that exact area, many years earlier was often discussed among those old enough to remember. Tradition held that the murdered man had been a Highland cattle drover returning home from the south; and that he had been killed for the substantial amount of money in his possession at the time.

It was the year 1695. The drover had arrived late at night at the Mains of Mause, hoping to push on towards the Estate of Roehalzie. As it was already dark, the drover stayed the night at the Mains of Mause; and left early in the morning. David Soutar, with his dog, accompanied the man on the pretext of showing him the road towards Roehalzie. Once they had reached a secluded spot, David Soutar then ordered his vicious dog to attack and kill the drover. When he was sure the body was lifeless, Soutar stole the drover's cash purse and quickly buried the body.

After committing the murder and disposing of the corpse, Soutar returned to his family's cottage at the Mains of Mause. His mother and father, rather surprised at his long absence and appearance, asked him what he had been doing. David Soutar did not answer, instead, he hurriedly packed his possessions and left. He was last seen by labourers in the Brae of Cochrage (sometimes known as Cochrage Muir) near to Stanley, as he hastily made his way south towards England.

William Soutar asked the apparition 'Why have you decided to trouble me now after all this time?' The spectre replied, 'Because, after I killed the man, yours was the first face I saw, as a bairn in your mother's arms.'

According to *The History of Blairgowrie*, written by John MacDonald in 1899, an old lady from Blairgowrie, who had lived towards the end of the 18th century, often claimed that:

The siller of the drover paid for the wood with which the west loft in the old Kirk of Blair was made.

When questioned, she would offer no explanation to her rather cryptic utterance. 'Siller' was an old Scots word for silver, probably suggesting that ill-gotten gains were involved in financing the building of the old kirk in Blairgowrie. Perhaps David Soutar, racked with guilt, donated some of the money he had stolen towards the construction of the church?

William Soutar, so thoroughly shaken by the ghostly encounter (which it transpired had happened on several previous occasions), wished for a formal record to be taken down. A reliable, first-hand account was thus transcribed by the Bishop Thomas Rattray, straight 'from William Soutar's mouth'. Thomas Rattray was a highly intelligent and respected man, who was to be appointed Bishop of Dunkeld shortly after this incident, and, in 1738, Primus of the Scottish Episcopal Church (the presiding Bishop for the entire Episcopal Church in Scotland). Bishop Rattray may be considered a reliable source, not easily swayed. Further credence may be added to the reliability of this account as, firstly, it is known that Bishop Rattray was in Blairgowrie at this time, and secondly, a written record of the document was kept. This manuscript lay lost, and forgotten, in Craighall House, Blairgowrie, for almost 200 years until it was rediscovered in the early part of the 20th century:

The following is the 'Account by William Soutar', from the original manuscript, written by Bishop Thomas Rattray, taken down at the time from William Soutar's mouth'. 1731:

In the month of December 1728, about the skysetting, I and my servant, with several others living in the same town, heard a skraiching (shrieking) *and I, following the horse with my servant a little way from the town, we both thought we saw what at the time we judged to be a fox, and hounded two dogs at it, but they would not pursue it.*

About a month after that, as I was coming from Blair alone about the same time of the night, a big dog appeared to me, of a dark greyish colour, betwixt the Hilltown and Knowhead of Mause on a ridge a little below the road. In passing me, I sensed it touch me on the thigh at my haunch bone, upon which I pulled my staff from under my arm and let a stroke at it, and I had a notion at the time that I hit it, and my haunch was painful all that night; however, I had no great thought of its being anything extraordinary, but that it might have been a mad dog wandering.

About a year after that (to the best of my memory in the month of December 1729), about the same time of the night and at the same place, when I was alone, it appeared to me again just as before, and passed by me at some distance, and then I began to have some suspicion that it might be something more than ordinary.

In the month of June 1730, as I was coming from the Claith (Cloth) Market in Perth, a little before skysetting, being alone at the same place, it appeared to me again and passed by me as before. I had some suspicion of it then likewise, but I began to think that a neighbour of mine in the Hilltown, having an ox lately dead, it might be but a dog that had been at that carrion, by which thought I endeavoured to put that suspicion out of my head.

On the last Monday of November 1730, as I was coming from Woodhead. a town in the ground of Drumlochy, it appeared to me again at the same place, and after it had passed by me, just as it was near getting out of my sight, it spoke with a low voice. I distinctly heard it say these words, 'Within eight or ten days, do or die', and it having uttered this, it then disappeared and no more words passed at that time.

On the morrow I went to my brother, who dwells in the Nether Aird of Drumlochy, and told him of this last and all the former appearances, which was the first time I ever spoke of it to anybody. He and I went that day to see a sister of ours in the Glen, who was a-dying, but she was already dead before we came. As we were returning home, I desired my brother, whose name is James Soutar, to go forward with me till we should be past that place where the dog used to appear to me, and just as we were come to it, at ten o'clock at night, it appeared to me again as formerly, and, as it was passing over some ice. I pointed to it with my finger and asked my brother if he saw it, but he said he did not. Nor did his servant who was with us. It spoke nothing at the time, but just disappeared as it crossed the ice.

On the Saturday night thereafter as I was at my sheep cotes putting in my sheep, it appeared to me again at daylight, betwixt dawn and skylight, and upon saying these words, 'Come to the spot of ground within half an hour', it just disappeared. Whereupon I came home to my own house and took up a staff and also a sword with me, off the head of the bed, and went straight to the place where it formerly used to appear, and after I had been there some minutes, and had drawn a circle about me with the staff, it appeared to me. I spoke to it, saying, 'What are you that troubles me?', and it answered me, 'I am David Soutar, George Soutar's brother; I killed a man more than five-and-thirty years ago, when you were but new-born, at a bush by the east side of the road as you go into the isle'. As I was going away, I stood again and said, 'David Soutar was a man, and you appear like a dog'. Whereupon it spoke again and said, 'I killed the man with a dog, and am made to speak out of the mouth of a dog and tell you, and you must go and bury these bones.'

Upon this I went straight to my brother's house and told him what had happened to me. My brother, having told the minister of Blair, he and I came to the Minister on the Monday thereafter.

About midnight on Wednesday 23rd December 1730, being in bed, I (William Soutar) heard a voice, but said nothing. The voice said, 'Come away'. Upon this I rose out of bed, cast on my coat, and went to the door, but did not open it, and said, 'In the name of God, what do you demand of me now?' It answered, 'Go, take up these bones.' I said, 'where shall I get these bones?' It answered again, 'at the side of a withered bush, and there are but seven or *eight of them remaining.' I asked, 'Was there anyone in the action but you?' It answered, 'No'. I asked again, 'What is the reason that you trouble me more than the rest of us?' It answered, 'Because you are the youngest.' Then I said to it, 'depart from me and give me a sign that I may know the particular place, and give me time to find this place.' The voice answered as if it had been at some distance from the door, 'you will find the bones at the side of a withered bush; there are but eight of them, and for a sign you will find the print of a cross impressed upon the ground.'*

On 29th of December, William Soutar, his brother, and seven or eight men met at 'The Isle'. Permission was granted by the landowner to disturb the ground and eventually, upon finding the right spot as indicated by the apparition, digging commenced around sunrise. Several human bones were found. The unearthing was witnessed by the Parish Minister, the laird, and approximately 40 villagers (who had gathered to witness the commotion).

The bush, just as depicted by the apparition was found to be withered about half-way down its trunk. And, as described, a sign was indeed marked on the ground about a foot from the bush. The sign was an exact cross, forming an 'X'. Each of the two lines being about 18 inches long and 3 inches wide, 'and impressed into the ground, to a depth of about an inch or two.'

William Soutar went on to explain that

When breaking up the ground at the bush we found the following bones, viz. the nether jaw with all the chaft (Scots dialect for jaw) *teeth in it, one of the thigh bones, both arm bones, one of the shoulder blades, one of the collar bones, and two small bones of the forearm.*

He concluded his statement by saying:

The bones were carefully wrapped in linen and placed in a coffin especially made by a wright for the purpose. We sent for the mortcloth (a ceremonial cloth, draped over the coffin) *and the remains were buried in a grave in the Kirkyard of Blairgowrie that same evening, just as the sun was setting.*

Many have since thought that William Soutar was merely labouring under a delusion, or that it was a trick played on him by one of his neighbours. Regarding the bones that were found, sceptics have theorised that they were likely to be the remains of a calf which had been buried there some years before. However, this does not explain how William Soutar knew the exact spot in which to dig for human remains, nor the fact that many people witnessed the disinterring of the remains, examined the bones, and were present at the burial.

At the time of John MacDonald's *The History of Blairgowrie*, written in 1899, there were certainly still many people in Blairgowrie who believed the story to be true. Enough to warrant the inclusion of the story in his book. The story was also given much credence by the *Dundee Evening Telegraph* during the 1930s, following the re-discovery of Bishop Rattray's original manuscript.

Interestingly, the story bears a remarkable similarity to the story of *The Unlikely Witness*, in one of my previous books, *Blood Beneath Ben Nevis*; and may well be an amalgamation of two legends which have been combined over time.

As for William Soutar, it appears that the ghost of his ancestor did not disturb him again. It was assumed by everyone that the spirit had been granted its request to rest in hallowed ground, breaking the spell. There were no further sightings of the strange apparition, and the people of Blairgowrie could now sleep safely in their beds once more.

THE CRAIGIE GLASSBLOWER

Monday 31ˢᵗ January 1910 was a cold and blustery day. Robert Duff had returned from work to his lodgings on the top floor of Craigie Bank House, in the high Craigie district of Perth. It was already dark.

Aged 23, and a glassblower by trade, Duff was sturdily built and strong, yet also small in stature, with a pale complexion and thinning hair.

Duff had married just four weeks earlier and immediately moved all his belongings into his new lodgings. His bride, Agnes, joined him shortly afterwards. Agnes already had a child, a four-year-old girl called Margaret Dougall, who resided with her mother's family in Carnoustie. Duff, however, agreed that the child could live with them, and his wife sent word to her family in Carnoustie that Margaret (or Maggie as she was known) would be sent for. A few days later the young girl arrived.

Maggie was a sickly child. Duff would later claim that the young girl was often prone to fits and colds. She was also inflicted at the time with a condition called 'bow leggedness' and required exercise, therapy, and patience on the part of her parents. Unfortunately, Duff was anything but patient. He was short tempered, lacked empathy, and struggled to deal with the demands of raising a child. Perhaps the arrival in Craigie of the four-year-old was difficult for a man who generally shrugged off the pleasures of companionship, like other men of his age, instead preferring solitude; or spending time alone looking after his pigeons and rabbits

In the early evening of 31st January (the same day that the infamous Dr Crippen is thought to have poisoned and buried his wife in the cellar of their London home) Duff and his wife sent for the doctor. On his arrival at their lodgings, they informed Dr W Fraser Bisset that Maggie had passed away while sat on Duff's lap. She was still sat, lifeless and in the same position, when the doctor arrived. Duff informed Dr Bisset that:

The girl was undergoing a fit and I tried to calm her. I sat Maggie on my knee, close to the fire, and tried to comfort her. Unfortunately, Maggie simply passed.

Dr Bisset took the child and laid her down on the bed to examine her. Perhaps to see if she could be revived, perhaps to begin the formalities of issuing a certificate. Agnes wept constantly throughout these proceedings.

However, on examining the girl's body, Dr Bisset was alarmed by his initial discovery. He refused to issue the customary death certificate, much to Duff's consternation. Instead, he immediately contacted Dr Parker Stewart (the Medical Officer of Health for Perth). Dr Stewart, in turn, ordered a post-mortem. The examination, carried out by Dr Stewart himself, assisted by Dr Stirling, revealed an alarming number of bruises all over the child's head and body. The doctors then informed the Procurator Fiscal who immediately ordered the arrest of Robert Duff.

Meanwhile, the Crown authorities ordered an immediate investigation into the death of Maggie Dougall. Interviews were carried out with neighbours, evidence was gathered, and Duff was charged as follows:

Robert Ford Duff, glass tubemaker, you are charged at the instance of the complainer that you did, on various occasions, between the 8th January 1910, and 1st February 1910, particularly on the nights of 28th January and 30th January, in your dwelling house, Craigie Bank House, and in a field in Craigie Road, assault Margaret Dougall, your stepdaughter, knock her down in said field, kick her, throw her over the fence of said field on to the street or road; throw her violently on to the floor of your dwelling house, and otherwise mistreat her, and did murder her.

A large number of people (reported as 'several hundred' by the local newspapers) attended Duff's bail hearing. Rumours in Perth were rife regarding the enormity of the crime, and many of the 'curiosity-mongers' jostled to witness for themselves the man accused of such a shocking murder. Bail was refused and Duff was remanded in custody in Perth awaiting trial.

Meanwhile the funeral took place of Maggie Dougall at Wellshill Cemetery in Perth. She was buried in a small, white coffin, bearing a brief description. No clergy were present, and no prayers were read.

Robert Duff's case opened before a packed court in Perth on Friday 1st April 1910. He was visibly shaken and could only answer the charge in a tremulous and almost inaudible voice, 'Not guilty, my Lord'.

The prosecution presented a comprehensive case in court. This included a large plan, on which were marked all the locations at which Duff had assaulted Maggie. The field in Craigie was clearly marked as 'C' on the map, and a witness was able to describe seeing Duff throwing his step-daughter over the wire fence, onto the road.

Next to be called were Agnes Dougall's mother, sister, and cousin, all who were able to explain the heart-breaking background to Maggie Dougall's upbringing. Agnes had given birth to Maggie in November 1905 at her sister's house in Carnoustie. Agnes was only 18 years old at the time and Maggie's father was a married man. He had refused to have anything to do with the child. Within two weeks of the birth, Agnes handed over her baby to her sister, Betsy, claiming she could not look after her. Betsy did consider adopting Maggie, but her real mother, Agnes, refused to hand over the birth certificate.

It appeared that Maggie was a healthy child at the time, and not prone to colds or fits, nor was she difficult or troublesome.

Agnes Dougall, who regularly sent five shillings a week toward the upkeep of Maggie, appeared by surprise at her sister's house on 9th January 1910, asking for her daughter to be returned. Agnes told her family that she had recently married and that her new husband had agreed to take in the child. Betsy Dougall refused to let Maggie go until she had met Agnes's new husband for herself. Agnes duly left, only to return the following weekend with Robert Duff. After a discussion, the family seemed satisfied that Duff would make a suitable stepfather to Maggie and the newly-weds left soon after, taking the girl with them. It was the first time Agnes had seen her daughter since leaving her four years earlier.

Betsy Dougall was also able to confirm to the court that Maggie, at the time she left Carnoustie, was in good health, had no bruises, had never had a serious fall, and was not prone to fits of any sorts. Betsy also told the court that she remembered Robert Duff enquiring whether Maggie was 'blasphemous at all'. The family replied that she was not. 'Good', replied Duff, 'I want to have the child baptised myself'.

The newly married couple seemed very happy, Betsy thought, although Agnes's family did think it odd that neither of them spoke to Maggie at all during their visit to collect her.

Once Maggie had moved into Craigie Bank House, her grandmother told the court, she went to visit her on two occasions. She noticed that there had been a marked decline in Maggie's health and appearance in just one week of living at her new home.

In the late evening of 31st January (following Dr Bissett's visit to attend to the dead child) Robert Duff and his wife Agnes went to visit Agnes's mother. Duff told her that the young girl had 'taken a fit and died'. Agnes cried throughout and her mother was unable to understand a word that her daughter said.

The newly married couple returned the following day and Duff informed Maggie's grandmother that there had been 'some trouble with the police and the body has been taken away to be examined'.

At this point in the trial the accused broke down and reached for his handkerchief. It was reported that he spent a large proportion of the remainder of the trial with his handkerchief held close to his eyes; or completely covering his face.

More damning still, though, was the evidence of Grace Gow, who occupied the apartment underneath Robert Duff in Craigie Bank House. She testified that in the early morning of Tuesday 25th January she was awoken by the sound of a thud from upstairs, followed by a cry. Her first thought was that someone had fallen out of bed. Following the commotion, she distinctly heard raised voices, but was unable to make out exactly what had been said. The next morning Grace Gow had intended to go upstairs and enquire exactly what had happened during the night, however there was no need. Robert Duff knocked on her door and abruptly asked:

Did you hear any row up the stairs this morning?

I did, Mrs Gow replied, *I thought it was someone falling out of bed*

No, answered Duff, gesturing upstairs with his right hand, *it was that little bastard up there, that would not sleep.*

Duff added that because he had wanted the child to sleep, the child had cursed him, so he had picked her up and thrown her across the room.

Mrs Gow, in horror, told Duff, *You might have broken her arms or her neck!*

Oh no, replied Duff, *I watched how I flung her.*

Mrs Gow reprimanded Duff, arguing that he could not possibly have seen where, or how far, he had thrown her in the dark. She chastised him further with a phrase that was widely repeated in the newspapers at the time, becoming a lurid headline, and which caused several editorials to pontificate on the abuse of children throughout the country:

YOU SHOULD NOT HASH HER!

(Hash means to attack or severely reprimand another person, either physically or verbally)

Mrs Gow's evidence to the court continued. On 28th January, Robert Duff again came downstairs and knocked on Mrs Gow's door. He entered, without waiting to be asked inside, and noticed Mrs Gow's daughter crying.

'What are ye crying about?' Duff asked her. He then added, in a rather chilling manner, 'Do you ever hear that one up the stair crying? She doesn't get leave to cry.'

The following day Maggie appeared with a swollen nose and scratched face. Duff told his concerned neighbour that Maggie had fallen over, due to the frost, and he had carried her home, by the heels, holding her upside down. Mrs

Gow told Duff she thought the swelling was very bad. Duff replied that he had squeezed Maggie's nose hard to force out the bruised blood. This seemed a cruel and painful thing to do to a child, Mrs Gow thought, and left in disgust.

On Sunday, 30th January, a series of loud bangs and thuds were heard from the Duff's flat. After much crying and shouting, the noise subsided. On the morning of her death, Duff told Mrs Gow that Maggie had fallen down the stairs on the previous evening.

However, the following evening the flat upstairs seemed to be unusually quiet. Mrs Gow thought to herself that the child may well be asleep. At 9.20pm, her rare evening of peace was shattered when Agnes knocked on her door; crying, she exclaimed 'my bairn is dead!'

Mrs Gow immediately went upstairs and asked Duff, 'Why did you not send for me or call a doctor?'

'There was no need of it', Duff replied. He explained to Mrs Gow that Maggie had been 'in a fit' for four hours and that he had sat with it. When Mrs Gow asked why Maggie was not in her nightclothes Duff explained that after Maggie had died, he had removed her nightclothes and re-dressed her in her ordinary clothes. Duff said that he had then washed her nightclothes in hot water. Mrs Gow also noticed a mark on Maggie's face, which Duff said had been caused by her falling onto the fender.

The defence tried to convince the court of Robert Duff's good character. He seemed a quiet man. Fond of pigeons and rabbits, he also read a lot, and seemed of above average intelligence. Duff's sister claimed that she had never seen Duff abuse the child and that he was a good father.

However, the defence could not overcome the evidence offered by John Auld of Eden Terrace. He was walking home on 28th January and noticed a man on the west side of Craigie Road. As he got nearer, Auld noticed the man striking something in the long grass beside the road. As he got within a few yards of the man (who he identified in court as Robert Duff), he was able to observe Duff knock the girl down, then kick her three times. Maggie cried out, a sound which sickened John Auld. It sounded like a dog whining, he told the court. Duff, on noticing John Auld, then quickly dragged the child off in the direction of Windsor Terrace.

Dr Parker Stewart reported to the court on the full details of the post-mortem, which revealed the catalogue of injuries suffered by Maggie during her two-week stay at Craigie Bank House. Maggie had suffered multiple bruises and cuts to her body and face. The doctor was of the opinion that death had been caused by a particularly violent blow to the head, causing damage to the brain. He also thought that the injuries, including the swollen eyes, could not have been caused by a fall. Distressingly, it also appeared that Maggie had not eaten for several days.

Duff's defence could provide no convincing counter evidence and Robert Duff was found guilty of murder and sentenced to death by Lord Low. Despite a plea for mercy put forward by the jury, the execution was arranged for 10th May. The crime was described by Lord Low as the 'fiendish work of a man without a heart'.

A crowd of several thousand people gathered outside Perth Courthouse and, at one stage, stormed the building in order to gain access. There were several injuries and the police were forced to restore order.

The case caused a sensation in Perth, shocking the inhabitants of the city. Yet the story did not end there.

Public distaste for the death penalty was growing and a petition was put forward to the Secretary of State for Scotland, citing the Jury's original recommendation for mercy and Duff's apparent quiet and sober nature. Duff denied, and continued to deny, the murder charge. His health suffered in Perth Prison during his long wait for an answer to his petition for leniency. Some members of the public signed the petition. Some, however, believed a rumour that circulated the fair city at the time. It was suggested that Duff's crimes towards Maggie Dougall were so horrific that some of the evidence had been heard behind closed doors and never disclosed to the jury or courtroom. This was denied by the authorities, and Duff's reprieve was eventually granted. His sentence was reduced to Life Imprisonment with hard labour

He was transported to Peterhead Prison, near Aberdeen, on 28th June 1910, to serve out the rest of his sentence. By the end of September Duff's family began to fear for his life. He suffered greatly under the hard regime of prison labour and discipline. A near brush with death, coupled with his fragile mental state, saw Duff deteriorate markedly. His family and other campaigners for the mental health of prisoners wanted him transferred to Perth Prison. However, this was felt to be too insensitive in a city still shocked by his crime. Duff was eventually transferred to the District Lunatic Asylum at Murthly to regain his reason.

Meanwhile, solicitors debated whether, if Duff was to regain a degree of sanity, should he be returned to Peterhead Prison to complete his life sentence or remain at Murthly. He was, after all, still only 24 years of age.

In a final twist to the story, Duff's mental health improved to a level at which the authorities deemed him well enough to be transferred back to Peterhead Prison. Once there, his duties were less onerous, Duff was given employment in the prison bakehouse. Eventually he was released, following a period of good behaviour, in November 1927, after serving 17 years of his sentence.

Duff moved to the Rutherglen area of Glasgow and secured employment. He even occasionally visited his family in Perth. Still aged only 40, he lived out the rest of his life peacefully. It is not known if he ever visited the grave of Maggie Dougall, the stepdaughter, whose life he had ended within just two weeks of meeting her.

Agnes Dougall, it is believed, emigrated to the USA following the Great War.

CAMP 21: COMRIE'S WARTIME SECRET

The majority of people would probably be shocked to know exactly how many German prisoners were housed in Britain during the Second World War.

The numbers swelled as the tide of the war began to turn in the Allies favour. By late 1944 as many as 400,000 were kept in prisoner of war camps up and down the country (largely without the knowledge of the general public, for fear of causing panic and stoking any fires of retribution). Among these 400,000 men were housed a large number of prisoners deemed 'dangerous die-hards'. As many as 70,000 of whom had taken a sacred blood oath to fight for the Fuhrer until their death. However, kept most secret of all from the general population, were the soldiers singled out from among these 70,000 men to be the most fanatical and dangerous of all - 4,000 elite veterans of the SS. Soldiers who, quite simply,

refused to believe that Hitler's vision of a Third Reich was over. These men were designated 'category black prisoners' and sent to Cultybraggan Prison Camp at Comrie, in the tranquil surroundings of Perthshire. This camp was then codenamed 'Camp 21'. The real nature and identity of the prisoners incarcerated there was labelled top secret and never revealed to those living locally.

These men, despite being Hitler's most dedicated ruthless and well-trained troops, were openly marched from the train station to the camp, often with groups of young children from Comrie Primary School running alongside them. One local man would later recall:

We often used to walk up Drummond Street and Dalginross alongside the prisoners. They used to sing as they marched and we picked up a song or two.

As autumn turned to winter during 1944 the population of Perthshire anxiously tuned their wireless sets into the BBC Home Service, as news of the German counter-offensive in Europe filtered through. Yet, unknown at the time, the German military were planning a simultaneous counter-offensive right here in Britain.

However, the initial planning of this secret operation did not begin in Comrie, among Hitler's elite SS guards, but over 400 miles away at another prisoner of war camp at Devizes in Wiltshire. Ultimately, however, it would lead to the terrible incident at Camp 21 on Saturday 23rd December 1944.

An audacious plot was hatched among a group of fanatical

Nazis POWs at the Devizes camp. The soldiers intended to break out, then steal weapons and vehicles and liberate fellow German prisoners from another nearby camp. This daring plan was intended to cause panic among civilians leading to a snowball effect, as the men moved hastily from camp-to-camp freeing more and more POWs. It was hoped this would eventually lead to a full-scale German counter-offensive attack on London, coinciding with a secretly planned German attack from across the Channel.

It appears that one of the less fanatic German POWs at Devizes, Feldwebel Wolfgang Rosterg, may have informed the Allies of the plan, forcing it to be aborted. He and the thirty ring leaders of the plot were subsequently transferred to the Comrie camp on 17th December 1944.

Rosterg stood out among the other hardened Nazis and SS soldiers at Camp 21. He was in his early thirties, wore glasses and was the son of a wealthy German industrialist. Rosterg was well travelled, spoke numerous languages, and had been a successful businessman in his own right before the outbreak of war. Unfortunately, these characteristics had made it easy for him to be labelled as an outsider by the most fervent Nazis imprisoned alongside him.

Rosterg had become disillusioned with Hitler and the Nazi regime and had openly told his fellow POWs that 'he was not a filthy Nazi like them.' His ability to speak English perfectly was treated with suspicion by his fellow prisoners, who felt certain he was a traitor to the Nazi cause. Indeed, even before being captured by the British, Rosterg has realised the hopelessness of the German Army's situation.

He was recorded as saying:

It was only after discussing the situation with a German soldier that I realised a Hitler victory would not even have been desirable. I went off my job on September 3rd, I abandoned everything, and hid in the woods.

On being captured by the Allies he immediately turned informer, telling British intelligence officers about the location of the German Army's nearby ammunition dumps and troop dispositions.

It is almost certain that his fellow POWs at Camp 21 believed that Rosterg was an informer and a traitor to The Third Reich. On his arrival at Camp 21 he was asked by the other inmates, 'Are you a National Socialist?', to which he replied, 'I am not, I most certainly am not!'

This simple reply from Rosterg was enough to begin the inexorable chain of events that commenced at 6.30am on the morning of 23rd December 1944.

Shortly after the 6.30am morning roll call at the camp, a band of eight of the most hardened Nazi POWs, grabbed Rosterg from behind, as he made his way back to his room. They quickly pulled him into hut number 4 without the prison guards noticing. Rosterg's fate had already been decided by the desperate group, who had met in secret the previous day and opted to dispense their own form of justice. Each of the eight men believed they had the right, governed as they were by their SS oath of loyalty, to hold their own 'kangaroo court', in which they would be acting as judge, jury, and executioner.

Sturmmann Kurt Zuehlsdorff, Unterofflizier Rolf Herzig, Matrozer Josef Mertens, Unterscharführer Joacim Goltz, Obergefreiter Herbart Wunderlich, Rottenführer Heinz Brueling, Oberfähnrich Erich Pallme Koenig, and Oberfeldwebel Hans Klein were all staunch supporters of Hitler and, even at this late stage of the war, still believed a German victory was inevitable.

The men produced a rope they had secreted earlier and placed it around Rosterg's neck. As the rope was pulled tighter and tighter, the eight men questioned him at length about their aborted escape attempt at the Devizes Camp. Had he informed the British? Was he a traitor to the Third Reich? He was beaten with an iron bar, which had been removed from the stove. He begged for mercy, but his pleas fell on deaf ears. Rosterg's answers were largely ignored as four of the men beat him so savagely that his face soon became unrecognisable.

Shortly before 8am the men removed the rope and dragged Rosterg to another empty hut (sometimes used as an office by the compound leader). One of the group, Erich Koenig, informed Rosterg that, 'If you had any honour, you would hang yourself'. Rosterg replied, 'I am not able to do it'.

The rope was then secured tightly around his neck for a second time, and he was pushed through the office door and onto the compound outside. Meanwhile, a sizeable crowd had gathered outside, drawn by the commotion. They struggled to recognise Rosterg, due to his bloodied, bruised, and swollen face. One end of the rope was seized by Joacim Goltz, so that Rosterg could not escape, and he was thrown to the ground. Lying prone on the floor, he was then savagely kicked, beaten, and stamped on in a vicious act of revenge for his disloyalty to the Reich.

Some of the onlookers who had witnessed this atrocity attempted to wash the blood from Rosterg's face, but the gashes bled profusely, and their efforts were in vain. However, they were pushed aside by his attackers. Four of the group then took hold of the rope and dragged Rosterg from the clearing in front of the compound office, towards the lavatory block. Rosterg's bloodied body was dragged over an asphalt path with large kerbstones. As they dragged him along the path his head was deliberately smashed against the kerbstones. He was then hauled through the mud until he was absolutely black and completely unrecognisable.

Once behind the closed doors of the lavatory block, Goltz and Zuehlsdorff threw one end of the rope over a pipe which ran around the ceiling, and Mertens pulled hard on the other end. However, he was unable to pull the body up by himself and called out for assistance. Three of the group then hauled Rosterg into position until, finally, their ultimate bloody vengeance was extracted on the man they believed had wronged them.

Mercifully, a later examination of Wolfgang Rosterg's body by a doctor revealed that he was almost certainly dead at this point. Regardless of that, the men left his body hanging, lifeless, from the ceiling of the lavatory block.

The British Authorities seem to have been slow in investigating any incidents at the camp. Had they been quicker perhaps they might have saved Wolfgang Rosterg. Just a week earlier, the body of another German prisoner, Oberleutnant Willy Thorman, had been discovered hanging from a tree at the camp.

Attitudes to prisoners of war and degrees of punishment were very different during the Second World War than perhaps they might be today. The eight men who had brutally beaten and executed Wolfgang Rosterg were investigated and eventually arrested by Major RAL Hillard, of the Judge Advocate General's Office. They were charged as follows:

That you have committed a civil offence, that is to say, murder, in that you did at Comrie on December 23rd 1944, murder Prisoner of War No. 788778 Feldwebel Wolfgang Rosterg.

The men were transferred to a military court in London, comprising of six British officers and a Deputy Judge Advocate General in full wig and gown. There was no jury present at their hastily arranged and secret trial. A military solicitor, appointed by the army, represented four of the accused, and a barrister the other four. Two British captains were employed as interpreters during the trial, although (it later transpired), little was explained to the men; and they understood almost nothing of the proceedings. Standing strictly to attention, during the opening formalities, each of the accused men pleaded not guilty to murder.

Captain Willis, in charge of the men's defence, emphasised that the accused Nazis who had murdered Rosterg believed it was the proper end for a traitor, and not a crime within the bounds of wartime practices. Through Captain Willis, the eight accused men informed the Military Court that, in 1943, an attempt to escape had been made and planned by British officers in a prison camp near Breslau. That attempt was eventually aborted, however, as the plan had been revealed to the German prison camp authorities by a British officer at the camp. That officer had, in turn, been hanged by his fellow British POWs, and the German authorities took no steps to punish the men responsible, recognising the act as a justifiable one.

The court sat for 10 days and, because the hearing was a secret military one, the trial was not reported in the press until after the final sentence had been pronounced. The men were given the option to speak before their sentence was carried out, but they all stood stiffly to attention and shouted 'Nein!' Five of the men were sentenced to death, including Koenig who was the most senior, and deemed to be the most dangerous, two had their sentences commuted to life imprisonment, and one was acquitted.

One month and four days after the end of the war, on the morning of Saturday 6th October 1945 at Pentonville Prison in London, the sentence was carried out. It was, perhaps, the only occasion in British legal history that five men were hung on the same day, for the same crime. Although the war was now over, the wounds were still raw, and feelings ran high among the general population. No reprieve was offered to any of the men (despite the cessation of hostilities). No protesters or mourners gathered at the prison gates (as was customary). In the usual manner following an execution, a notice was placed on the prison gates at 10.30am, which simply stated:

We, the undersigned, hereby declare that judgement of death was this day executed on Kurt Zuehlsdorff, Joseph Mertens, Joachim Goltz, Heinz Brueling, and Erich Pallme Koenig in His Majesty's Prison of Pentonville in our presence'

Signed – Colonel F. Forbes, Deputy Provost General
Ben Grew, Governor of the prison
Ronald George Smith & Clifford Howell,
RC Chaplains to the forces

In another example of the strength of public opinion at the time, the newspapers reported the story, liberally mocking the men's' inability to speak or understand English. Following their execution, the banner headline simply read 'Five Huns Hanged'

The body of Wolfgang Rosterg was buried at Cannock Chase German Military Cemetery in the Midlands, alongside all the German servicemen who had died in Britain during the course of the war. In a bizarre coincidence the adjacent grave to Rosterg was that of the other Camp 21 casualty, Oberleutnant Willy Thorman, who had been found hanging from a tree just a week before Rosterg's death.

Camp 21, or Cultybraggan Camp, near Comrie, unlike many other camps, was not broken up after the war. In 2007 it was purchased by the local community. Part of the original camp has been renovated and is now open to the public. Covering more than 90 acres, it is one of only three preserved POW camps surviving in the UK. Even today, the Nissen huts remain largely unchanged, as a visible reminder to visitors of the sinister events that occurred there during December 1944.

Finally, and in a tragic twist of fate, recent research has unearthed the possibility that Wolfgang Rosterg was not, in fact, the informer who had told the British authorities of his fellow prisoner's planned escape from the Devizes POW Camp. That appears to have been another, unidentified, officer.

MI5, the branch of British Intelligence tasked with 'turning' German prisoners and spies, had hoped to utilize Rosterg's anti-Hitler feelings and his language skills. They had transferred him to Camp 21 at Comrie as a 'mole', hoping to glean some vital information about the proposed German secret offensive.

Whether knowingly or unknowingly, they almost certainly condemned Rosterg to his fate.

THE MOTIVELESS MURDER
(PART ONE)

In the city of Perth, on the night of Saturday 19th August 1944, the public houses were unusually busy. News of the advance into Paris by the combined Allied Forces had been broadcast that evening on the BBC Empire Service news. The liberation of the French capital had begun, and the pubs were full as the people of Perth joined in the celebrations.

Mary Latimer had agreed to meet her mother at the Auld Hoose Inn on the corner of King Edward Street and South Street. Mary, who was 29, had recently married a soldier named Joseph Sweeney. However, he was now away on active service in the Far East. Mary, who still tended to use her maiden name Latimer, worked as a maid at a nearby hotel and as a waitress at a tearoom in St John's Place. After a tiring day at work, she was now looking forward to meeting her mother, Grace Fleming, for a drink. The pair found a corner table and, making themselves comfortable, sat drinking and laughing.

Around 8.45pm a young man approached their table. He made no pretence at good manners, but simply interrupted their conversation, saying to Mary, 'What about that shilling you owe me, then?'

Before the man could speak again, or Mary could answer him, her mother Grace asked the man, 'Where's your accordion, then?'

She recognised the man as a ploughman, or farm worker of some sort, and the comment was a derogatory reference to the popular entertainer of the period, Jimmy Shand, a ploughman who played the accordion.

There was an awkward silence, followed by a cackle of laughter, from those stood close by. Suitably embarrassed by the comment, the man returned to the bar, glancing furtively at Mary as he did so. It did not appear to Mary's mother, Grace, or to anyone else in the public house, that Mary had recognised the young man, or had met him before.

The landlord, Duncan McDougall, remembered serving him, and would later recall this in court. The man asked for 'two bottles of Guinness and two 'nips' of gin', which were decanted into an empty bottle. The man indicated to the landlord that he wished to take the drinks away with him. He then went outside into the cool night air.

Meanwhile, back inside the Auld Hoose Inn, Mary Latimer stood up, clearly the worse for drink, and put on her red coat and yellow scarf. Surprised by her daughter's sudden movement, her mother asked her, 'Where are you going?'

'I'll be back in a wee while', Mary answered and, with that, she left the Auld Hoose Inn, went outside onto the street, and out of sight of those still inside the pub.

At the same time, Police Sergeant William Gardner was off duty and stood chatting with two friends, on the corner of Horner's Lane and South Street. It was approximately 9.15pm. A young couple walked past him, heading down Horner's Lane in the direction of Canal Street. Sergeant Gardner would later testify to the court that the young lady 'appeared to be under the influence of drink.' The man seemed to be sober, however. Sergeant Gardner recognised the young lady as Mary Latimer, as the family were familiar to him. He did not recognise the man.

Another witness, Mary Jackson, saw the couple as they passed her in Horner's Lane. She also recognised Mary Latimer and spoke to her. Mary Jackson went one step further than Police Sergeant Gardner and said, 'in my impression, Mary Latimer was very drunk.' She, too, did not recognise the man.

Mr Charles Law was sitting in the doorway of his house at 41 Canal Street, as the couple passed him. He noted the time as 9.23pm on the clock outside the Co-operative building opposite.

Meanwhile, close by, Mr David Proudfoot was standing outside 93 Canal Street. Even at that late stage of the war, he was on fire watching duty for the night. Mr Proudfoot also noticed the couple, as they passed him in the street. He described the man as 'wearing a cap, blue sports jacket and flannels, and he had a bottle of stout in his jacket pocket.'

Mary Latimer reached into the man's pocket, pulled out the bottle of stout, and offered it to Mr Proudfoot. He thankfully received it and promised to drink it later, as he wanted to keep a clear head while on fire watching duty. The young couple then carried on walking, hand-in-hand, before turning into Canal Crescent, and out of Mr Proudfoot's line of sight. Canal Crescent is a narrow, curving road of cottages and workshop premises, fronting directly onto the street.

Two further witnesses (who would also later be called in court), Mrs Mary Donaldson and Mrs Mary McLaren, both saw the young couple continue along Canal Crescent before turning out of sight and into the open passageway entrance at 117 Canal Crescent, where a Mr David Wilkie owned a sewing machine workshop on the first floor. One of the two lady witnesses, Mrs Mary McLaren, watched carefully from her kitchen window opposite, as the couple disappeared into the shadows of the passageway. She also thought the young woman appeared to be very drunk, or perhaps even ill. Mary McLaren put the time at just after 9.20pm.

A few minutes later, about 9.30pm, the man appeared again from the shadows of the passageway, this time alone. He spoke to a boy who was leaning against the red pillar box in Canal Crescent, then returned, back through the doorway of 117 Canal Crescent and out of sight of Mary McLaren once more. Ten minutes later, around 9.40pm, Mrs McLaren, who was still watching from her kitchen window, witnessed a man exit hastily from the building, moving very quickly in the direction of Scott Street. However, she was unable to state positively that it was the same man that had entered the passageway with Mary 20 minutes earlier.

Following that, peace and quiet returned to Canal Crescent; and Mrs McLaren retired to bed.

The following morning, Sunday 20th August 1944, Mr David Wilkie, the owner of the sewing machine business on the first floor, arrived early at 117 Canal Crescent. It was 8.30am. Mr Wilkie's business premises were upstairs, and as he attempted to push the door open, he noticed a pair of bare legs on the floor behind the door. Then, as he pushed the door a little further ajar, to his horror, he saw the body of a young woman slumped on the floor. He immediately summoned the nearest police officer, Constable George Ross, who entered the premises first, with Mr Wilkie stood behind him. The two men were shocked to discover the body of Mary Latimer lying twisted on the floor, her head and shoulders resting on the first stair, soaked in a pool of blood. Her head and face were covered in cuts and gashes, and a smashed Guinness bottle lay next to her body. There was broken glass on the floor and around the neck of the victim, knotted tightly, was a blood-stained yellow scarf.

An immediate murder investigation was launched, headed by Deputy Chief Constable George Jack. Such was the severity of the crime, and, to help alleviate the concerns of the city's population, it was felt that a senior officer should handle the case.

George Jack's team of officers immediately questioned witnesses and households within the city centre and were soon able to build up a picture of the man's movements on the previous evening. Although the face of the victim had been rendered unrecognisable by the ferocity of the attack, the police were quickly able to make an identification. Grace Fleming, on hearing of the discovery of a body in Perth city centre, had feared that the victim may have been her daughter, as Mary had failed to return to the Auld Hoose Inn on the previous evening.

Grace Fleming was able to give the police a full description of the man in the blue sports jacket and flannels, who had approached their table in the public house the previous evening and spoken to her daughter Mary. This seemed to match the description of a man observed by several witnesses later that same evening walking arm-in-arm with Mary along Canal Street.

Further witnesses also came forward, who all reported seeing a man, matching the same description, later in evening, around 10.50pm, at the Reliance Garage in South Street, Perth. This time, however, he was riding a bicycle and apparently heading for a dance at the village hall in Forteviot, a few miles outside Perth – a journey of some 35 minutes by bicycle. After cycling to the dance, the man was seen there between 11pm and 11.30pm by several members of the public, who all would later identify him as Douglas Smith, aged 24, a local farm labourer.

At the dance Douglas Smith apparently met his friend Stewart Christie, and the two men returned to their lodgings together, at Windyedge Farm, just off the Glasgow Road, shortly after midnight.

The following morning (Sunday 20th August) Stewart Christie was surprised to see Douglas Smith awake early, cleaning the flannel trousers and shoes he had been wearing the previous evening, with a damp cloth which he had dipped in petrol. It seemed a little odd to Christie, but he did recall he had seen Smith cleaning a dirty mark from his clothes in this way before.

Meanwhile, the description of the man last seen with Mary Latimer was circulated to all those present at the Forteviot dance, who all recognised the man as Douglas Smith. Importantly, none of these witnesses could remember seeing Douglas Smith at the dance any earlier in the evening than approximately 11pm. Smith's name was soon passed to the Perth police. Deputy Chief Constable George

Jack and two burly constables called at Windyedge Farm, at 10pm on that Sunday evening. Smith was asleep in the bothy at the time. One of the constables shone his torch in Smith's face, while the other grabbed him by the arms. Before Smith could wrestle himself free; he was greeted with the words, 'Douglas Smith? I am arresting you in connection with the murder of Mary Latimer in Canal Crescent, Perth. Get dressed, you're coming with us.'

Smith looked incredulously at the police officer and replied, 'What, me?' The police also searched the room and took away Smith's suit for examination, as well as a pair of brown shoes which were drying outside on the windowsill, having been cleaned by Douglas Smith earlier that morning.

He was questioned for several hours at Perth police station, and an identification parade was subsequently arranged. Two witnesses were able to confirm that Smith was indeed the man they had seen leaving the Auld Hoose Inn just prior to Mary Latimer, and he was formally charged with her murder. Interestingly, however, Smith was not identified from the police line-up by a single witness as the man seen walking arm-in-arm with Mary later that evening.

Two days later, on Wednesday 23rd August, public interest in the case reached fever pitch in Perth. Large numbers of onlookers attended Mary Latimer's funeral at Wellshill Cemetery in the city. Even more tried to squeeze into the Courthouse, as Smith appeared before Sheriff Valentine at his preliminary hearing, all desperate to catch a glimpse of the killer.

Douglas Smith pled not guilty to the charge of murder and his trial date was set for November 14th, 1944, at the High Court in Perth.

Lord Albert Russell was to be presiding judge at the trial. Public interest was intense, and the courtroom was packed. Smith's indictment was read out to the court:

Douglas Smith, you are charged that you did on the 19th day of August 1944 murder Mary Latimer, or Sweeney, in premises at 117 Canal Crescent by striking her on the face with a bottle and tying a scarf round her neck and that you did strangle her contrary to common law.

Perth police had taken a great deal of care with their accumulation of the forensic and medical evidence in the case. Scotland's most experienced forensic experts were called to give testimony in court. They had painstakingly examined the jacket and trousers taken from Douglas Smith, as well as the clothing and corpse of Mary Latimer. In 1944, of course, it was not possible to provide an exact DNA match of blood, hair or fibres taken from the victim's clothes or body. However, it was possible, by use of a powerful microscope, to distinguish human blood in clothing and, at least, detect similarities in fibres, materials, hair, etc. Douglas Smiths' flannel trousers did show a small trace of blood on the knee, and the jacket contained a slight smear of blood on the inside of the right sleeve. The brown shoes, worn by Douglas Smith, both had bloodstains on the instep, despite having been cleaned. Adhered to the dried blood were red fibres that appeared to be similar to those taken from the deceased woman's red coat.

The broken glass on the floor next to Mary Latimer's body, and imbedded in her wounds, was identified as being from a Guinness stout bottle, like the one sold to Douglas Smith at the Auld Hoose Inn, and similar to the bottle noticed by witnesses in the jacket pocket of the man walking along Canal Street with Mary Latimer.

Coupled with the evidence of several witnesses who had observed a man matching Smith's description with Mary Latimer in Canal Crescent, and the telling evidence that Smith had been seen washing his clothing on the morning following the murder, it seemed a watertight case to prosecuting attorney Mr GR Thomson KC The defence objected at this point, reminding the jury that despite several witnesses describing the man seen walking with Mary as similar in appearance to Douglas Smith, none had actually been able to pick him out at the police line-up.

That concluded the evidence for the prosecution.

Meanwhile, Douglas Smith continued to protest his innocence throughout the trial. His defence was led, with much passion, by one of the country's leading defence counsels Mr James Latham Clyde KC (Clyde would later become Lord Advocate, then Lord President for Scotland, as well as the member of parliament for Edinburgh North).

Smith always maintained that he had left Mary Latimer outside the Auld Hoose Inn talking to a foreign airman, possibly Canadian, and that she 'had gone off with him', as Smith put it. Smith also claimed that he had never met Mary prior to that night, and that they had chatted for some time at the traffic lights outside the pub, but that they had not walked off together. Smith stated to the court that he had eventually left Mary outside the pub, talking to the airman, not around 9.15 to 9.30pm, as most of the witnesses had testified, but an hour later, at about 10.30pm. His claim, however, does not seem to have been taken seriously by the court.

Smith's defence team cross examined the forensic evidence, questioning the blood traces found on the accused's clothing. Close attention was drawn to the fact that despite the huge amount of blood found at the crime scene, and on the victim's clothes, face and body, Smith's clothes only revealed two tiny blood stains and one small smear on the sleeve. This did not seem to match the evidence taken from the crime scene. Surely, it was argued, such a violent assault would have resulted in both parties becoming covered in blood? Mr James Latham-Clyde addressed the jury, saying:

There is no doubt that some man must have left that stairway with his coat and cuffs reeking with the blood of that woman. If he really had committed this crime and proceeded to tie a scarf around her neck and strangle her, it was inevitable that his clothes would have been covered with blood. The woman's own clothes were soaked in blood. Surely, they would have found Smith's clothes in the same condition? His clothes were examined by the best expert the Crown could muster in Scotland. And what was the result? They found only one or two spots, which were absolutely insufficient to account for the crime.

Smith's barrister then produced a further witness who testified, under oath, that a few days prior to Mary's murder

Smith had cut his knee, whilst bathing in the river, and that this was far more likely to account for the small amount of blood found on his trousers, rather than the vicious attack in Canal Crescent.

Several acquaintances of Smith's were produced in court, some that had known him for years, and they all testified to his pleasant and placid nature. In fact, no one could remember Smith ever losing his temper before, even if he had taken a drink. He was generally thought to be of good character and had no previous convictions. Smith's barrister looked the members of the jury directly in the eye and said:

If you really believe Douglas Smith murdered this poor girl, there must have been some sudden change in his whole nature. Something totally unexpected must have taken place on that stairwell to account for this incident. The only explanation was that some other man must have intervened between the time the accused left the premises and the time she met her death.

The elderly lady, Mrs McLaren, who had observed, from her kitchen window, Mary Latimer and her apparent killer entering 117 Canal Cresent, was shown the bloodstained coat that Mary had been wearing on the night of her murder. She failed to identify it. She also stated that she thought the man she had seen with Mary was both older and stouter than Douglas Smith.

The statements of these witnesses, and the complete lack of any apparent motive, were also called into question by the defence, who then rested their case.

Lord Russell summed up the case for the jury, reminding them that the evidence of the red fibres found in the dried blood was 'by no means conclusive', and that 'you must not convict on this evidence alone. Neither must you allow any personal sympathies to interfere with your decision making.'

The jury were also reminded by Lord Russell:

That no fingerprint evidence was available at the scene of the crime, which might have proved the prisoner's guilt beyond any doubt. As this was not available, you must remember that it is not up to the defence to prove their client's innocence, but merely to provide enough doubt in his guilt. If, you, the jury, feel that such a doubt exists, you are duty bound to find the defendant not guilty, or at the very least, his guilt not proven. If, however, you feel the evidence presented here proves his guilt beyond any reasonable doubt, then you must find him guilty.

Douglas Smith continued to protest his innocence, as he was led away. Lord Russell instructed the jury to retire and consider their verdict.

THE MOTIVELESS MURDER
(PART TWO)

The jury in the case of Douglas Smith took just 30 minutes to reach their verdict.

Upon returning to their seats, a hushed tone enveloped the court room. Lord Russell asked the foreman of the jury if they had reached a verdict. He replied, 'Yes, your honour, we have'. The verdict was handed to the clerk of the court, who in turn handed it to Lord Russell. After carefully reading the piece of paper, the verdict was read aloud to the silent court room, 'Guilty'.

The jury, however, made a unanimous recommendation for mercy in the case (Scottish juries often requested a prison sentence or hard labour, as a substitute for the death penalty). Nevertheless, Lord Russell was unmoved, and no such plea was granted, as he slowly donned his black cap:

Douglas Smith, the sentence of this court is that you will be taken from here to the place from whence you came and there be kept in close confinement until the 12th day of December, and upon that day that you be taken to the place of execution and there hanged by the neck until you are dead. And may God have mercy upon your soul.

Smith was led shaking from the dock to be returned to his cell to await his execution.

Ultimately, it seems, the strange behaviour of Douglas Smith, following the murder, played heavily against him. Rising early on the Sunday morning to wash his clothes and shoes in petrol, the description of his distinctive blue sports jacket, and the imbedded blood and fibres in his clothing, were enough to persuade the jury. Despite a warning from Lord Russell, in his summing up, that the evidence of the fibres was 'by no means conclusive', and the continuing protestations of innocence by Douglas Smith, the jury, it seems, was not to be swayed in its conviction of his guilt, even though its recommendation had been that the sentence be commuted to one of imprisonment instead of execution.

An immediate appeal was lodged by Smith's barrister, James Clyde KC. The Scottish Court of Criminal Appeal met in Edinburgh on 5th December to hear Smith's case reviewed. A petition of 12,000 signatures for his reprieve had been gathered and was handed to the Appeal Court. James Clyde argued that Lord Russell had misdirected the jury, during his summation, that there was an element of doubt in the conviction, and that the evidence did not conclusively point to Smith as the murderer. He reminded the appeal court that the last witness to see Mary Latimer alive, the elderly Mrs McLaren, had not been able to identify Mary's coat when shown it in court, and that she had the impression that the man she had seen in Canal Crescent that night was much older and stouter than Douglas Smith. However, the appeal failed to move Lord Russell, Lord MacKay, and Lord

Stevenson, who concurred with the original verdict, stating that they had 'no doubt that the original jury were entitled to bring in the verdict that they did'.

The date for Smith's execution was set for December 23rd 1944, two days before Christmas.

Smith's story does not end there, however. The campaign for mercy in his case grew. More and more people signed the petition for leniency in the case and a plea was made directly to Thomas Johnston, the Secretary of State for Scotland. Eventually, just seven days prior to Smith's appointment with the hangman, the Secretary of State granted a stay of execution, commuting Smith's sentence to one of penal servitude for life. Smith was given the news in his cell by Baillie Burnside, the senior magistrate for Perth. Smith was greatly relieved by the reprieve and wept openly. Despite his obvious relief, he continued to protest his innocence as he was removed to begin his life sentence at Parkhurst Prison on the Isle of Wight.

However, two questions still remain - was Douglas Smith guilty of Mary Latimer's murder and did he receive a fair trial?

Firstly, the decision to stage the trial in Perth, and not at a more neutral venue such as Edinburgh, was certainly not in Smith's favour. Tensions in Perth were undoubtedly running high at the time.

The circumstantial evidence in the case was undeniably damning; but does seem to raise more questions than answers. Why did Douglas Smith continue to protest his innocence? His odd behaviour in rising early the following morning to clean his clothing and shoes with petrol, certainly points to a guilty man attempting to hide the evidence of his crimes. But why not simply destroy, hide, or throw the clothing away? And why attend the dance wearing the same clothing, which may have been spotted with blood which Smith might not have been able to see in the dark? And the important point that Smith's friend Stewart Christie had informed the police that he had previously seen Smith cleaning his clothing with petrol, so perhaps this behaviour was not as unusual as it first appears.

Smith's claim that he had parted from Mary Latimer later in the evening, was never believed or investigated. Had he really left Mary at around 10.30pm, leaving her talking to the Canadian airman? If he had done so, sightings of Smith at the Reliance Garage in South Street at 10.50pm, corroborates his version of events. The garage is just a few minutes from the Auld Hoose Inn. After all, logically, should there not have been many sightings of Smith, on a busy Saturday night in the centre of Perth, if he had actually left Mary at 9.40pm (as the prosecution claimed), but was still in the city centre at 10.50pm? There were no reported sightings of him between those times.

If, on the other hand, he had killed Mary at approximately 9.30pm (just after the last confirmed sighting of her), and he was indeed the man seen leaving Canal Crescent in a hurry at 9.40pm, why would he have stayed so close to the scene of the murder for a further hour and twenty minutes, until 10.50pm? Why not simply leave for the dance in Forteviot immediately, thus helping to establish an earlier alibi? There seems to be no logical reason for a murderer to stay within 200 yards of the murder scene and risk the chance of being witnessed or apprehended.

The prosecution argued that Smith had attended the dance in the hope that witnesses would assume he had been there all night, thus providing him with an alibi. However, if he really had hoped to achieve as early an alibi as possible, why not simply head for Forteviot immediately after the murder, instead of waiting another hour and ten minutes before leaving Perth?

No one at the dance could remember Smith being present prior to approximately 11.30pm. This does seem to corroborate the testimony of witnesses who remembered seeing a man matching Smith's description leaving Perth around 10.50pm. However, none of these witnesses, nor anyone at the dance, noticed any blood on his clothing either. The pathologist who examined the body of Mary Latimer the following day was unable to confirm the time of death to within anything less than a four-hour window. Therefore, Mary could feasibly have been killed at any time between the last sighting of her at 9.30pm and 1.30am the following morning, by which time Douglas Smith was tucked up in bed.

Furthermore, the police were so convinced that they had found the guilty man that no search was ever made for the mysterious foreign, possibly Canadian, airman; nor for any other suspect. Smith, in fact, from prison later told the police that it was possible that the airman could have been Polish, as it was difficult for him to understand the accent.

At that time, in 1944, Perth was awash with serviceman from all across the world, as the invasion of Europe intensified. The claim does not appear to have been investigated either.

The fact that Smith had purchased two bottles of Guinness and some gin from the Auld Hoose Inn, and that the man seen walking with Mary Latimer had a bottle protruding from his jacket pocket, is indisputable. However, it was common practice for men leaving a public house to purchase a bottle or two to take home with them. In 1944, the existence of late night off-licensed premises was extremely rare, and most men who intended to carry on drinking once they had left the pub were required to take their supplies home with them. Hence the expression; 'one for the road'. We know that one bottle of Guinness was handed to Mr Proudfoot, and one was smashed at the crime scene – but what happened to the bottle of gin? This was not found at the crime scene, and not noticed protruding from his pocket by any of the witnesses (as the Guiness bottle had been). Nor was it recovered on Douglas Smith's person when he was arrested; or located at his lodgings.

The various sightings of a man, seen walking arm-in-arm with Mary, were crucial in obtaining Smith's conviction. Yet he always denied this point, claiming that he had left her talking to a foreign airman outside the public house. Perhaps the pivotal piece of information that led to his conviction was the description of Smith obtained from witnesses who recognised him from *inside* the Auld Hoose Inn; and then picked him out at the formal identification parade. No positive identification of Smith was obtained from any of the witnesses who had only observed a man walking along the street arm-in-arm with Mary. It is also worth noting, it was now past 9pm and the blackout was still in force – there would have been no streetlights, neon shop signs, or bright car headlights. Surely, any witness sightings under those conditions should not have carried the weight in court that they did. Particularly when the burden of definite proof rests with the prosecution in a capital crime.

In fact, if Smith had not already freely admitted to standing and talking to Mary outside the Auld Hoose Inn, it might have been difficult for the prosecution to prove, beyond reasonable doubt, that Smith had actually met Mary at all, after leaving the pub. Remember, not a single witness could confirm the man seen with Mary was definitely Douglas Smith. It is also worth mentioning that if Smith had really murdered Mary, why admit to talking with her outside the pub, but deny walking away with her? Why not just refute all the allegations, since only denying one accusation appears suspicious and cagey?

Eyewitness accounts are notoriously inconsistent, of course. Only one witness mentioned that the man seen walking with Mary wore a cap. Crucially, the final witness to see Mary Latimer alive, Mrs McLaren, was not at all certain that the man she had seen walking with Mary in Canal Crescent, or leaving the premises in a hurry, was Douglas Smith at all. In fact, her impression was that the man was 'older and stouter'. Because of her age, 75, and the fact that her description did not match that given by others, it appears to have been conveniently ignored. The judge at the trial, in his summing up for the jury, stated that perhaps, 'Mrs

McLaren was so taken up with the appearance of the girl that she did not pay much attention to the man.' Yet she was the *only* witness who actually spent a sustained period of time, 10 minutes, observing the couple from her kitchen window.

No corroborating witnesses could be found to prove Smith's story, that he did not actually leave Mary until 10.30pm, when she began chatting to a foreign airman at the traffic lights outside the public house. Surely, on a busy Saturday night, it should have been possible to confirm his story. Just how determined the efforts of the police were to check Smith's account of the events is not known. Yet, why would he invent such a story? If he had completely fabricated his version of events, why not just claim that they parted company at 9.20pm instead, therefore placing some distance between himself and the brutal murder. Why choose 10.30pm? It makes no logical sense. And, if Smith did murder Mary around 9.40pm, where was he for the next hour and ten minutes, until he was next sighted at 10.50pm at the Reliance Garage?

Another baffling point, which does not seem to have been properly investigated, is why the couple walked to a dark and quiet street, in the opposite direction from Mary's lodgings in the High Street. It seems to imply a lovers' tryst, and that Mary already knew, or at least felt comfortable, with her companion on that evening.

If the man with Mary wasn't Douglas Smith, then perhaps it was a pre-arranged liaison with someone else? After all, she certainly would not have walked to Douglas Smith's lodgings, which were over seven miles away, and, besides,

Smith had a bicycle. Which leads to the curious evidence of the bicycle. Not a single witness mentioned that the man seen walking with Mary between 9pm and 9.30pm that night was also pushing a bicycle. If this man was Douglas Smith, then where was his bicycle during this time? And, if Smith was the mysterious man seen with her, why would he not simply have taken the bicycle with him from outside the Auld Hoose Inn as he strolled along the street with Mary? The route taken by the couple was, after all, in the general direction that Smith would be travelling later that evening. If the man spotted walking with Mary was indeed Douglas Smith, and he had left his bicycle outside the Auld Hoose Inn that night, he would have needed to double back on himself to collect it, adding needless extra time to his journey. This important inconsistency was ignored by the prosecution and the police, not mentioned by the defence, and thus not considered by the jury.

Finally, perhaps, the single most baffling aspect of the case is the complete lack of motive for the murder of Mary Latimer. None was ever found. She had not been robbed or sexually assaulted; and had walked willingly into Canal Crescent that fateful night. But, as Lord Russell explained to the court during the original trial, it is not incumbent on the prosecution to prove a motive, in order to secure a conviction.

In the case of Mary Latimer, no motive has ever been found. As a result, Douglas Smith served his sentence and was eventually released in the early 1960s. He lived a quiet and uneventful life, before passing away in 2012 at the age of 91.

Finally, there are three footnotes to the case. One rather sad, one intriguing, and one rather chilling.

Firstly, and rather poignantly, at the time of Mary's murder in 1944, her husband, Joseph Sweeney, had recently been killed on active service in the far east. The news of his death had not yet reached Mary, in Perth. She did not know of his death as she prepared to enjoy her Saturday night out, and, equally, Joseph would never have been aware of her flirtations with another man, or of her tragic murder. Joseph had been killed by the Japanese while serving with the 2nd Battalion of the Black Watch in Burma at the end of July, and he is now buried at Taukkyan War Cemetery in Myanmar.

Secondly, despite the usual ruling that the full record of the trial should be become available for public viewing after 75 years, the details of this case have been sealed for an additional nine years; and will not made available until 2028. No official reason has been given.

Finally, there is one obvious question that should be asked. If Douglas Smith did not kill Mary Latimer, then who did? The police, so certain that they had their man, never looked for another suspect. After some in depth research I discovered at least nine serious assaults on young women took place in the centre of Perth between March 1944 and July 1946. All the attacks involved the victims being beaten around the head with heavy objects. Although not all the assaults cannot be attributed to the same perpetrator, one incident stands out from the rest. In July 1946, two years after the murder of Mary Latimer, a man attacked another young women named Rose Miller, in an act of revenge. He later told the police, 'she said she would be faithful to me, but I discovered that she was going from place to place and flirting with other men. Therefore, I decided to hit her.'

Why might the attack on Rose Miller be related to the case of Douglas Smith? After all, Smith was now safely locked away in Parkhurst Prison. However, the incident carries some chilling parallels with the Smith case. In a similar fashion to Mary Latimer, Rose Miller had been hit over the head with a heavy object (probably a bottle) and left for dead. Fortunately, she recovered and was able to identify the man. His name was Lance Corporal Maximillan Worczwk, a Polish soldier who had been stationed near Perth for some time. He was arrested after a police chase and imprisoned. Perhaps, most remarkably of all, the attack took place at exactly the same house as the murder of Mary Latimer two years earlier – 117 Canal Crescent. Worczwk had taken Rose Miller there, perhaps already knowing that the stairwell would be empty and out of sight. Even more astonishingly, Mrs Mary McLaren, the elderly lady in the house opposite, observed Worczwk leaving the property in a hurry, and described him to the police as being similar to the man she had seen two years earlier following the murder of Mary Latimer. Lance Corporal Worczwk plead guilty to the assault and was imprisoned. As far as I have been able to ascertain he was never questioned about the murder of Mary Latimer.

REMEMBERING PERTHSHIRE'S WITCHES

The extent of the persecution of witches in Scotland in general, and in Perthshire in particular, is staggering to our modern sensibilities. Recent research by the University of Edinburgh has uncovered records detailing the execution of anywhere between 4,000-6,000 witches in Scotland from the 15th century until the mid-18th century. It seems there were certain passages of time in which public paranoia reached a crescendo, mainly following the passing of the Witchcraft Act in 1563. During these periods, hundreds of witches were persecuted and tortured.

Remembering that Scotland's population at the time was less than one million people, the rate of persecution far exceeded that in England, where approximately 500-1000 witches were killed, or in northern Europe. Approximately 90% of those executed were women.

King James VI of Scotland's visit to Denmark, where witch-hunts were already common, in 1589 seems to have been instrumental in increasing the fervour of the phenomenon in Scotland. After his return to Scotland, he attended the North Berwick witch trials, the first major persecution of witches in Scotland under the 1563 Act. Several people, most notably Agnes Sampson and schoolmaster John Fian, were convicted of using witchcraft to cast storms against the King's ship.

King James became obsessed with the threat posed by witches and subsequently set up royal commissions to hunt down any witches in his realm, recommending torture as the only way to deal with suspects. He is also known to have personally supervised the torture of women accused of being witches. Inspired by his personal involvement, in 1597 he wrote the *Daemonologie*, a tract that opposed the practice of witchcraft and which provided background material for Shakespeare's *Tragedy of Macbeth*.

King James employed both witchfinders and witch prickers, who travelled from community to community in the lucrative business of witch-hunting. During the height of the witch trials during the 16th and 17th centuries, common belief held that a witch could be discovered through the process of pricking their skin with needles, pins, and bodkins (a daggerlike instrument for drawing ribbons of blood through hems or by punching holes in cloth).

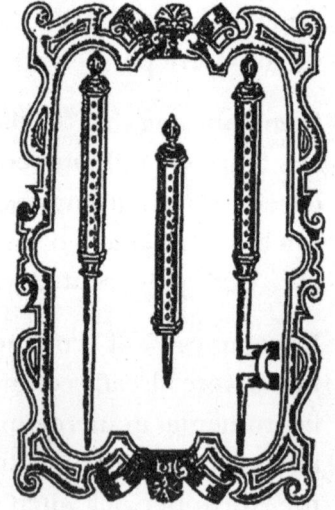

This practice derived from the belief that all witches and sorcerers bore a witch's mark that would not feel pain or bleed when pricked. The witch prickers earned a handsome reward for each witch caught, and employed several resourceful tricks, including needles that concealed the blood drawn from the alleged witch, thus meaning the poor victim could be accused of witchcraft even if blood had actually been drawn.

A confession extracted by torture was considered the best method of obtaining the truth from an alleged witch; and was frequently used. In England, witches were hanged. In Scotland, victims were strangled, then burned at the stake.

Yet despite the prolific and sensational nature of witch trials in Scotland there are very few physical monuments to mark their suffering still visible today. However, here in Perthshire we are lucky to have three very different memorials to their suffering, all of which can still be visited today.

The first monument takes the form of the 'witch's stone'. Travelling along the A822 road towards Crieff, just before Gilmerton, there is a small road on the right leading to Monzie and the Famous Grouse Experience. After two hundred yards you reach the large gatehouse for Monzie Castle on the left. Ask at the gatehouse and they will point you to the stone, in the field about 300 yards after the Monzie stone circle and 200 yards past the gatehouse itself. The standing stone is said to mark the site of Kate McNiven's execution. Known as the 'Witch of Monzie', she was thrust in a wooden barrel and rolled down the steep hill on the north side of the Knock of Crieff, before being burnt. The hillside is still marked on maps as Kate MacNiven's Crag.

Kate had been the nursemaid to the Graeme's of Inchbrakie, and was accused of witchcraft, including the spell of turning herself into a bumble bee.

During the 16th century it was customary to take your own cutlery with you when invited to eat at another household. Whilst attending such a meal, the Laird of Inchbrakie was infuriated by a bumble bee buzzing around him. Eventually, he managed to catch the bee and stood up to put it out of the window. Upon his return to the table he discovered, to his astonishment, that his knife and fork had vanished from the table. Together with his servants he searched the house thoroughly without finding them. To his surprise, when he returned to the estate at Inchbrakie, the missing knife and fork were sat in their usual place. In those paranoid times, the only plausible explanation open to those present was that Kate McNiven had used her powers of witchcraft to transform herself into a bumble bee, whilst simultaneously transporting the Laird's cutlery back to Inchbrakie House; then changing herself back into human form, all before his return to the estate. The idea that he had simply forgotten to bring his knife and fork with him in the first place does not seem to have been entertained.

This, together with a succession of other inexplicable events, galvanised the authorities into action. Kate was arrested and brought to court. Following a declaration of the 'evidence' she was tried and convicted of witchcraft. Her punishment was proclaimed for all to hear - strangulation and burning. Her arms and legs were then tied, and she was dragged up the north east face of the Knock of Crieff, to the top of the steep cliff. Here she was rolled down the precipitous cliff in a wooden barrel. Once at the bottom, still just alive, but no doubt suffering from horrific injuries including many broken bones, she was tied to the stake and firewood piled up around her. The Laird of Inchbrakie, when he heard of the planned execution, rushed to the scene and pled in vain for her to be set free.

Kate noticed the Laird in the crowd and called out for him to come towards her. As he did so, she lowered her head and bit off a blue bead from her necklace, spitting the bead into his outstretched hand. Kate declared loudly to the gathered assembly that provided the family, 'kept the stone in Inchbrakie House itself, the house would be there for ever more'. The stone was then set in a golden ring and kept as Kate had instructed. The ring was kept in a small jewellery box and only daughters-in-law were permitted to touch it. Many years later, in the mid-19th century, it appears that, while all the family were abroad, one of the family's descendants, Patrick Graeme, removed the ring and took it outside the boundaries of the estate. Just a few years later the Graeme's were forced to sell much of their land, and, within a generation, the family were ruined and their ancient ancestral home of Inchbrakie House was demolished.

The exact date of Kate MacNiven's trial is not known. However, recent research seems to indicate 1568 as the date. If so, it would make poor Kate one of the earliest victims of the 1563 Witchcraft Act.

We now move to the south of Perth and Kinross, to the peaceful village of Crook of Devon, about four miles to the west of Kinross. Visiting today, it is hard to believe this was once the scene of the infamous killing of a coven of so-called witches, which took place in the summer of 1662. Detailed accounts of the witches' trials have survived in the *Proceedings of the Society of Antiquaries of Scotland*; and can still be read online. The court met on five different occasions at Tullibole Castle to decide the fate of the terrified suspects.

At the first trial the accused were Agnes Murie of Kilduff, Bessie Henderson of Pitfar and Isabella Rutherford of Crook of Devon. After a detailed investigation, they were unanimously convicted. The following sentence was passed:

All three taken away to the place called Lamblaires, bewest the Cruik Miln (Mill), *the place of their execution, tomorrow being the fourth day of this instant month of April, betwixt the hours of one and two in the afternoon, and there to be stranglit to death by the hands of the hangman, and thereafter their bodies to be burnt to ashes for their trespass.*

William Donaldson was named as the 'doomster' (executioner) who would carry out the awful sentences.

At a second trial, three weeks later, five witches were accused, each who had been incriminated by the first three as having been present with them at their alleged meetings with the devil (it was common practice for convicted witches to accuse others, as it potentially offered them an escape from the death penalty). This time the accused were the warlock, Robert Wilson of Crook of Devon, Bessie Neil of Gelvin, Margaret Lister of Kilduff, Janet Paton of Crook of Devon and Agnes Brugh of Gooselands. All met a similar fate and were executed the next day.

Ten days later, two further witches were accused, 'Margaret Hoggin, relict (old Scots dialect for widow) of Robert Henderson, and Janet Paton of Kilduff, relict of David Kirk'.

Margaret Hoggin was apparently reprieved, owing to her age – she was 79 - but for Janet Paton there was no escape, and she was strangled and burned 'between four and five o'clock in the afternoon', immediately following her trial, on a mound in Crook of Devon (close to where the village hall now stands). Alexander Abernethie was recorded as the 'doomster'.

More than two months would pass before the next trial was held, apparently because the remaining members of the coven had fled in terror. However, on 21st July, two further prisoners were brought to trial; Janet Brugh, wife of James Morels, and Christine Grieve, wife of Andrew Beveridge. Janet was convicted and executed the following morning while Christine was acquitted, only to be re-tried and convicted by the same jury on 8th October. She also was 'stranglit and burned by Thomas Gibson, doomster, five days later between the hours of two and three o'clock in the afternoon'.

Why were so many people accused in such a small community? Several reasons have been suggested for these convictions. Evidence against them was probably concocted by malicious neighbours, and confessions could have been obtained by keeping the accused in darkness and solitary confinement, without food, until they hallucinated, as was often the case. There was certainly a frightening paranoia surrounding witchcraft and the power of Satan at this time.

Today the little hillock of Lamblaires can still be seen in a field beside Crook of Devon, its tranquil appearance concealing the dreadful scenes that once took place here. However, for those wishing to visit, a very different kind of monument exists to the victims of the Crook of Devon witch trials. A memorial to the 11 people executed for witchcraft was unveiled in 2012 at Tullibole Castle, location of the sensational trials, and former home to William Halliday who was responsible for the persecution of the 'covens' in the village during the 17th century.

The Witches Maze at the castle was the idea of Lord Moncrieff, who now owns Tullibole. He was inspired to commission the maze as no memorial exists in the village to the witches' suffering. The finished memorial maze is circular, 33m (100ft) wide and consists of 2,000 beech trees. At its centre is a 1.5-ton elaborate sandstone pillar, with the names of the victims etched on it.

In addition to this modern monument to the persecution of witches, there also exists in Perthshire a much older and more mysterious memorial. It is one of very few known memorials anywhere in Scotland and is particularly interesting as it names not only the date of her execution, but also her name, the enigmatic 'Maggie Wall'.

Next to the B8062, just outside the small village of Dunning, near to Auchterarder and nestled in the former parklands of Duncrub Castle, lies an unusual and striking monument. This collection of stones stands 20 feet high and is topped with a cross. It bears the following words in stark white lettering, 'Maggie Wall burnt here 1657 as a witch'.

A mystery has always surrounded the identity of Maggie, with experts on witchcraft in Scotland doubting if she ever existed at all. No record of anyone named Maggie Wall is contained in *The Survey of Scottish Witchcraft*, an online resource which charts every recorded witch trial between 1563 and 1736. What is known, however, is that six other women from the parish of Dunning were arrested and accused of witchcraft in July 1662. Three of them, Isobel McKendley, Elspeth Reid, and Jonet Toyes were strangled and burned following the trial, in front of a local panel of commissioners. Their co-accused, Isobel Goold, Agnes Hutstone, and Anna Law, appear to have been set free.

In addition to there being no details of a woman named Maggie Wall ever being tried as a witch, a mystery also surrounds the date of the monument itself. Despite the structure carrying the date '1657', there was no record of the monument itself existing prior to 1866 (where it first appears on an Ordnance Survey map). However, during research for this book, I unearthed a reference to the memorial in the *Perthshire Advertiser*, dated 20th September

185,–this is the oldest reference to Maggie Wall yet discovered. The article, a guide to country walks, seems to give the impression that the monument was well established at that point and states:

Journeying westward, and about half a mile from Dunning, we see over the policy wall on a rising ground among the trees, a monument not to be met with in any other town. It is rudely picturesque, and bears on it the short but emphatic description, "Maggy Walls (sic), *burnt here, 1657, as a witch". Alas, what a commentary on the times, when such atrocities were regarded by all as doing God's service.*

It is the earliest known reference to the monument. More recent preliminary dating of the stones seems to indicate the structure is no older than the beginning of the 19th century.

Some locals theorize that a member of the Rollos, a powerful family that lived in Duncrub Castle, had an affair with Maggie Wall and built the monument out of guilt.

The most plausible candidate seems to be a local man named David Balmain. He was a schoolteacher, a tenant of multiple farms, and a builder involved in the construction of many local buildings. The cross on the monument is re-cut from a house lintel-stone – strongly suggesting the work of a builder. Importantly, he was also the tenant of the field called Maggie Walls from 1797 onwards, which matches the archaeological evidence pinpointing the date of the monument's construction and style. It seems that the memorial was most likely constructed as a testament, either to the Dunning witches, or a combined memorial to all the witches murdered in Scotland during the witch-hunts, as no other such monument exists. A recently uncovered map from 1829 includes a reference to a forest, that formerly surrounded the location where the monument now stands, called Maggie Walls Wood. The wood no longer exists; and the cairn is now surrounded by open farmland. Perhaps the name was simply taken from the surrounding wood to represent the countless and forgotten women who were killed?

Even today, a visit to the monument continues to mystify and intrigue visitors. The cairn is often covered with pennies, feathers, candles, and other trinkets, left by anonymous visitors. A mysterious wreath is still occasionally laid on the monument, although it is not known when, or by whom. Attached is a card which simply reads, 'In memory of Maggie Wall, Burnt by the Church in the Name of Christianity'.

As recently as 2018 the monument was sealed off by the Perthshire police, while investigating a murder, and, perhaps most chillingly of all, it was revealed during their trial in 1966, that the notorious Moors Murderers, Ian Brady and Myra Hindley, had become fascinated with the monument and visited the site. Ian Brady even took a haunting photograph of Myra leaning against the stones, in which she stares disturbingly at the camera. There is an undeniably disconcerting atmosphere surrounding the monument, even for those who visit today.

ACKNOWLEDGEMENTS AND REFERENCES

Once again, this book would not have been possible without the continued encouragement and help of Kevin & Jayne Ramage and the Watermill Bookshop in Aberfeldy. Thank you for your enduring support. I would also like to express my gratitude to Ellen McBride, Alexa Reid, Perth & Kinross Library Archives, Aberfeldy Museum, Innerpeffray Library, Lara Haggerty, Melanie Bonn, Linda Sinclair, Pitlochry & Moulin Heritage Centre, Highland Archive Centre, Killin Heritage Society, and to all the family and friends that have encouraged my endeavours.

The following sources of information have also been invaluable in either helping to piece together the stories contained in this book, or for kindly supplying their permission for the reproduction of images and text: Aberfeldy Community Library, AK Bell Library, Highland Archive Centre, Scotland's People, Ordnance Survey, Aberfeldy Museum, The Royal Society of Edinburgh, National Census Archive, The Gazetteer for Scotland, Family Search, Find My Past, Police Scotland Archives Scotland, Commonwealth War Graves Commission, Electric

Scotland Database, Office for National Statistics, Imperial War Museum, National Library of Scotland, Scottish Database of Witch Trials, Dunning Village website, Tour Scotland, Survey of Scottish Witchcraft, BBC News Archive, Strathearn Local History website and group, Mapping Memorials to Women in Scotland project, Visit Scotland, Aberfeldy Museum, the British Newspaper Archive, DC Thomson, and the following newspapers and journals: *The Evening Telegraph, Oban Times, The Scots Magazine, The Press & Journal, Inverness Courier, Dundee Evening Telegraph, Dundee Courier, Perthshire Advertiser, The Scotsman, Edinburgh Courant, Vancouver Star, The Evening Post, Aberdeen Weekly Journal, Liverpool Echo, Daily Record, The Sun, Daily Express, The People's Journal, The Weekly News, Daily Telegraph, The Guardian, Glasgow Herald, The Northern Warder, Belfast Telegraph, Sunday Post, Sunday People,* and *Liverpool Daily Post.*

Bibliography of published resources used:
Jacobites by Jacqueline Riding, Letters of Rev. EJ Simmons and Beaumont Featherstone, *Scottish Ghost Stories* by James Robertson, *Historic Scenes in Perthshire* by William Marshall, *Waverley's Novels* by Sir Walter Scott, *The Scottish Witch-Hunt in Context* by Julian Goodacre, *The Road To Rannoch* by T Ratcliffe Barnett, *Witchcraft in Kenmore (1730-57)*, by John Christie, *The History of Blairgowrie* (1899) by John MacDonald, *The Jacobites in Perth* by Kathleen Lyle, *Perthshire Murders* by Geoff Holder, *No Fair City* by Gary Knight, *Who Killed Janet Smith* by Ed Starkey, *The River Runs Red* by Mark Bridgeman, Wikipedia, BBC History Archive, National Records of Scotland, *Whisky Smuggling* by Stuart McHardy, *Annals of Auchterarder and Memorials of Strathearn (1899)* by

ACKNOWLEDGEMENTS AND REFERENCES

AG Reid, *History of England* by Lord Macauley, *The Sheep Stealer* by The Wayfarer, *The Witch Cult in Western Europe* by Margaret Alice Murray, *Perthshire in History and Legend* by AC Mckerracher, *Behind The Barbed Wire* by Jane Middleton-Smith, *The First World War* by John Keegan, *Hidden History* by Gerry Docherty, *The Perthshire Book* by Donald Omand, *The Guide to Mysterious Perthshire* by Geoff Holder, *The History of Crieff* by Alexander Porteous.

TIPPERMUIR BOOKS

Tippermuir Books Ltd is an independent publishing company based in Perth, Scotland.

PUBLISHING HISTORY

Spanish Thermopylae (2009)

Battleground Perthshire (2009)

Perth: Street by Street (2012)

Born in Perthshire (2012)

In Spain with Orwell (2013)

Trust (2014)

Perth: As Others Saw Us (2014)

Love All (2015)

A Chocolate Soldier (2016)

The Early Photographers of Perthshire (2016)

Taking Detective Novels Seriously: The Collected Crime Reviews of Dorothy L Sayers (2017)

Walking with Ghosts (2017)

No Fair City: Dark Tales from Perth's Past (2017)

The Tale o the Wee Mowdie that wantit tae ken wha keeched on his heid (2017)

Hunters: Wee Stories from the Crescent: A Reminiscence of Perth's Hunter Crescent (2017)

A Little Book of Carol's (2018)

Flipstones (2018)

Perth: Scott's Fair City: The Fair Maid of Perth & Sir Walter Scott – A Celebration & Guided Tour (2018)

God, Hitler, and Lord Peter Wimsey: Selected Essays, Speeches and Articles by Dorothy L Sayers (2019)

*Perth & Kinross: A Pocket Miscellany:
A Companion for Visitors and Residents* (2019)

The Piper of Tobruk: Pipe Major Robert Roy, MBE, DCM (2019)

*The 'Gig Docter o Athole': Dr William Irvine &
The Irvine Memorial Hospital* (2019)

Afore the Highlands: The Jacobites in Perth, 1715–16 (2019)

*'Where Sky and Summit Meet': Flight Over Perthshire –
A History: Tales of Pilots, Airfields, Aeronautical Feats,
& War* (2019)

Diverted Traffic (2020)

Authentic Democracy: An Ethical Justification of Anarchism (2020)

*'If Rivers Could Sing': A Scottish River Wildlife Journey. A Year
in the Life of the River Devon as it flows through the Counties
of Perthshire, Kinross-shire & Clackmannanshire* (2020)

A Squatter o Bairnrhymes (2020)

In a Sma Room Songbook: From the Poems by William Soutar (2020)

*The Nicht Afore Christmas:
the much-loved yuletide tale in Scots* (2020)

Ice Cold Blood (2021)

*The Perth Riverside Nursery & Beyond:
A Spirit of Enterprise and Improvement* (2021)

*Fatal Duty: Police Killers and Killer Cops:
the Scottish Police Force 1812–1952* (2021)

The Shanter Legacy: The Search for the Grey Mare's Tail (2021)

*'Dying to Live': The Story of Grant McIntyre,
Covid's Sickest Patient* (2021)

The Black Watch and the Great War (2021)

*Beyond the Swelkie: A Collection of Poems & Writings to
Mark the Centenary of George Mackay Brown* (2021)

Sweet F.A. (2022)

A War of Two Halves (2022)

A Scottish Wildlife Odyssey (2022)

In the Shadow of Piper Alpha (2022)

Mind the Links: Golf Memories (2022)

Perthshire 101: A Poetic Gazetteer of the Big County (2022)

The Banes o the Turas: An Owersettin in Scots o the Poems bi Pino Mereu scrievit in Tribute tae Hamish Henderson (2022)

Walking the Antonine Wall: A Journey from East to West Scotland (2022)

The Japan Lights: On the Trail of the Scot Who Lit Up Japan's Coast (2022)

Fat Girl Best Friend: 'Claiming Our Space' – Plus Size Women in Film & Television (2023)

Wild Quest Britain: A Nature Journey of Discovery through England, Scotland & Wales – from Lizard Point to Dunnet Head (2023)

Guid Mornin! Guid Nicht! (2023)

Madainn Mhath! Oidhche Mhath! (2023)

Who's Aldo? (2023)

A History of Irish Republicanism in Dundee (c1840 to 1985) (Rùt Nic Foirbeis, 2024)

The Stone of Destiny & The Scots (John Hulbert, 2024)

The Mysterious Case of the Stone of Destiny: A Scottish Historical Detective Whodunnit! (David Maule, 2024)

Salvage (Mark Baillie, 2024)

A Most Unsuitable Game: Celebrating Scottish Unsuitable Women's Football Fifty Years After the Ban (Karen Fraser, Julie McNeill & Fiona Skillen (editors), 2024)

FORTHCOMING

William Soutar: Collected Works, Volume 1 Published Poetry (1923–1946) (Paul S Philippou (Editor-in-Chief) & Kirsteen McCue and Philippa Osmond-Williams (editors), 2024)

William Soutar: Collected Works, Volume 2 Published Poetry (1948–2000) (Paul S Philippou (Editor-in-Chief) & Kirsteen McCue and Philippa Osmond-Williams (editors), 2024)

William Soutar: Collected Works, Volume 3 (Miscellaneous & Unpublished Poetry) (Paul S Philippou (Editor-in-Chief) & Kirsteen McCue and Philippa Osmond-Williams (editors), 2026)

William Soutar: Collected Works, Volumes 4–6 (Prose Selections) (Paul S Philippou (Editor-in-Chief) & Kirsteen McCue and Philippa Osmond-Williams (editors), 2027+)

The Black Watch From the Crimean War to the Egyptian Campaign (Derek Patrick and Fraser Brown (editors), 2024)

Drystone: A Gathering of Terminology and Technique (Nick Aitken, 2024)

The Scottish Murder Book: Sensational Scottish Murder Trials. Book 1: Perth, Angus and Fife (Mark Bridgeman, 2024)

The Lass and the Quine (Ashley Douglas (writer), Katie Osmond (illustrator), 2025)

The Royal Edinburgh Military Tattoo: 'The Show Must Go On' – Travels of the Tattoo Producer (Brigadier Sir Melville Jameson, 2024)

Balkan Rhapsody (Maria Kassimova-Moisset, translated from the Bulgarian by Iliyana Nedkova, edited by Cara Blacklock, 2024)

Button Bog And Other Voices & Treasures From A Traveller's Kist (Jess Smith, 2024)

A Wildlife Guide to Edinburgh (Keith Broomfield, 2024/5)

The Road to Mons Graupius (Alan Montgomery, 2024/5)

The Whole Damn Town (Hannah Ballantyne, 2025)

All Tippermuir Books titles are available
from bookshops and online booksellers.
They can also be purchased directly
(with free postage & packing (UK only) –
minimum charges for overseas delivery) from
tippermuirbooks.co.uk

Tippermuir Books Ltd can be contacted at
mail@tippermuirbooks.co.uk